Advance Praise for Broken Stronger

"If you feel like a square peg trying to be forced into a round hole at work, *Broken Stronger* is a must read. Even if you are relatively content in your job/life, Elena has written a thought-provoking book on being a better version of yourself."

– Theresa Myers

"You've been called to launch your vision, your dream… your destiny! But, for some reason or another, it still hasn't happened…you're stuck. Well, no more waiting, no more stalling, no more delaying! Straight up? No more excuses. Elena's got your back! Inside this book, you're going to find the step by step, take you by the hand, hold you by the heart, guide to becoming your own Broken Stronger Boss. In a nutshell, if you want a no holds barred, tell it like it is, recipe for success…that's completely seasoned with experience, encouragement, and a healthy dose of tough love… *Broken Stronger* is book is for you!"

– Lyly Gonoratskiy
Lead Strategist & Founder
Sahm Squared Marketing

"I'm so very excited for all of you that are going to have the opportunity to purchase Elena Zehr's *Broken Stronger*. Let me start off by saying that as an individual and a fan of Elena, it brings 1   l her

T0150777

with the ability to help not only myself, but others who are trying to succeed in the entrepreneurial world.

Her faith amazes me in that she continued to live her dream even in the midst of her own brokenness. With that being said, this goes to show me that anything is possible when you truly listen to the plans God has for your life.

Elena breaks down every step in her book as to what it takes, and she doesn't sugarcoat anything. At the same time she provides you with confidence in believing in yourself, so that you know, you can totally do whatever you set your heart and mind to!

One of the areas in the book that I really appreciated is the fact that she believes in everyone, and that no one is better than another. She also wants us to lock arms with one another, because let's be honest, it takes "a village," and we can make each other better by lifting one another!

Thank you, Elena, for your vulnerability and transparency. I am proud to know you, and I will continue to live my dream, and follow the plan God has for my life!"

– **Esther Brock**

"*Broken Stronger* is filled with sound wisdom mixed with wit and just enough humor to assist me in the serious truths, I thought I already knew! It made me realize how these steps are critical in believing in my purpose to my core, not just conditionally. I love how it gave me clarity in how to act on these truths – and how to Live It!"

– Katrina Clark

"After reading *Broken Stronger*, I felt so empowered! I love the easygoing nature of the author. The book was very simple to follow. Every chapter left me filled with motivation. Everyone can take something from this book no matter where you are at in your life. I highly recommend it for anyone that needs that push!"

– Angela Zepeda

"Elena Zehr's enthusiasm is contagious! An easy to read, faith-led guide to believing in yourself and making your dreams a reality."

– Debbie Oliver

"Elena's vibrant passion for others is genuine. If you have a burning desire to achieve your dreams, she's a guiding light for personal fulfillment. Not afraid to lean on faith and perseverance. She will set your mind on fire to 'spark' that purpose for your life!!!"

– Karen Wigent

broken
STRONGER

broken
STRONGER

*8 Non-Negotiable Steps to
Break Free and Become the Boss
of Your Own Life*

ELENA RODRIGUEZ ZEHR

NEW YORK

LONDON • NASHVILLE • MELBOURNE • VANCOUVER

broken STRONGER

8 Non-Negotiable Steps to Break Free and
Become the Boss of Your Own Life

Published in New York, New York, by Morgan James Publishing in partnership with
Difference Press. Morgan James is a trademark of Morgan James, LLC.
www.MorganJamesPublishing.com

ISBN 9781642798227 paperback
ISBN 9781642798234 eBook
ISBN 9781642799002 audio
Library of Congress Control Number: 2019953420

Cover Design by:
Rachel Lopez   www.r2cdesign.com

Interior Design by:
Melissa Farr   melissa@backporchcreative.com

Editor: Bethany Davis

Book Coaching: The Author Incubator

Morgan James is a proud partner of Habitat for Humanity Peninsula
and Greater Williamsburg. Partners in building since 2006.

Get involved today! Visit
MorganJamesPublishing.com/giving-back

My gorgeous angel in Heaven, this is for you!
Together we became…Broken Stronger.
I will always love you.

Table of Contents

CHAPTER 1

You're Not Crazy

Girl, let me just start out by saying you're not crazy for wanting different for your life.

Everyone has become content with settling. That is crazy!

Settling for less, settling for average, settling for complaining. That is crazy!

Staring at the clock emotionless day after day, watching it go *tick tock, tick tock, tick toc*k…that is crazy!

But you, no, you're good, even though it may not feel that way right now.

Let me guess, your days go something like this…

Alarm goes off and you wonder how you can be this tired already.

You get up and get yourself (and everyone else in your household) ready for the day.

You drive to work, turn on your computer, get your coffee, talk with your coworkers, and get busy.

You sit behind your desk and find yourself wondering how in the heck you ended up there. You sit there trying to remember what it was that used to make you so excited to go to work. You remember the days you would walk into the building thinking you were going to make a difference.

Today, you sit there feeling like you're going to scream. You wonder how you can possibly answer another email or attend another meeting and talk about the same frickin' problems you've been talking about for years.

Then you find yourself apologizing to your G.O.D. for not being grateful. You remind yourself you shouldn't complain. You beat yourself up for wanting more.

You try to refocus and get back to the tasks at hand and – well, what do you know? It's time to go home.

This is not called being crazy, my friend. This is called being tired of wasting your time.

You're tired of being confined to an imaginary box that you're giving permission to suffocate you. Tired of being surrounded by people who are completely content with complaining every day. Tired of feeling held back, ignored, and disregarded.

I know it seems like no one understands you – and you know what, they probably don't. Not many people are like you. Not many people want to change their situation. They would prefer to nag and complain about it rather than do work to change it.

Lucky for you, you're different.

You've always been different.

And for some reason, it's never been that big of a deal to you…until now.

You know where you are is not what you are meant to be, but when you try to explain your dreams to people, they look at you like they've never heard such a thing.

Dream? What's that? *Passion?* Where's that? *Purpose?* Girl, please.

People may not understand you, but that does not make you crazy for wanting more. You're just different.

For the record, dreams always come one or two sizes too big. They do this so you can grow into them. Dreams have a funny way of pushing you into your more. Aren't dreams clever little fellas?

But wait, there's more! Enter…internal conflict!

You're happy and thankful for everything you have. You know your G.O.D. has blessed you more than you deserve. So, you struggle with questions like, "Why should I want more? What is this something inside of me fighting to get out? Will it just go away?"

I mean, your family is good. Your husband is good. Everyone else is good, so why do you need to go and mess things up, right? Aha, that's called guilt and it likes to make a dramatic grand entrance.

Girl, you know why you need to go and mess things up. Because you feel lost and your smile is nowhere in sight. Because those who are closest to you are getting the grouchy, mad-at-the-world version of you. The version that has no energy.

You're no fun anymore! That's why you need to go and mess things up.

Just because you're older and more responsible, doesn't mean you should become stuck in a routine that society has laid out for you and forget who you are. You're different.

I remember the moment at my job when I realized (and literally told myself out loud because, yes, I am crazy), "This is not my desk. This is not the desk for me. This is not my chair. I shouldn't be sitting here."

True story!

You may not have said those exact words to yourself, but your story is the same as mine, and I'll be the first one to let you know that there is a happy ending waiting for you, if you want it.

Let me ask you something. As time goes on, do you find yourself becoming more and more quiet? Are you spending more time in your own head, maybe even just a little bit guarded?

That's normal, because you're a deep thinker.

I'm sure even growing up, not everyone understood why you were so serious all the time. You may have always felt odd, but the good thing is, it's now becoming clear to you why you've always been the serious one.

It's probably freaking you out to find yourself wondering, "Am I supposed to be my own boss?" *Who said that?*

The Broken Stronger Boss Lady in you said that. She's trying to make her debut, and you keep fighting her. Warning: she's stronger than you think.

Boss ladies are fierce. Just sayin'.

Think about it though. You have always followed through and performed at the highest level in everything you do. You are fierce.

Even now, you're still killin' it at your job. You know you are good at what you do. You have improved things tremendously, but you've reached a peak. You know there is a limit of where you can go and what you can achieve at your job, and that part sucks.

Bottom line, without a specific type of degree, you've pretty much reached the highest level that you can reach, and even though there is so much more in you to contribute, no one will even look at you.

OUCH! Sorry, did that hurt?

It's frustrating because you do not want to go back to college. You do not want to spend that kind of money only to learn the same thing as everyone else. You can't stand to be in a room full of people being told what to think, wondering, "How is this going to set me apart?"

It's not that you didn't continue your education, you just chose to continue it in a non-traditional way. You chose to educate yourself in the things that mattered most to you, and even though all the certifications you hold are the best of the best in the world, no one will listen to you and take you or your ideas seriously because you lack specific titles or certain levels of education.

Somewhere along the way, it's become a way of thinking that if you don't have a certain level of college education, you must not have your crap together. I don't agree.

In my experience, I've noticed that those who invest in focused learning and receive training by experts in their field are the ones who take their success to a whole new level. A level that isn't taught in a standard classroom.

Don't feel bad for questioning why, or if, you should go back to college to take more classes, especially if you feel you'll be wasting precious time and money on things you will never use.

Instead, be proud of the degrees or certifications you do hold, including the specialties you've developed over the years.

Those count for something!

I'm on your side. I know you have good ideas. You know you have good ideas. It bothers you that no one will give you a frickin' chance. I'm here to tell you, my friend, that you don't need anyone to give you chance. Create it for yourself.

Look at all you've done. Be proud of all that.

Here's the thing. The feeling you have of being stuck is knowing that where you are is no longer where you want to be.

What you are doing is no longer the right fit for you.

You're not in alignment anymore, and you can tell. Don't ignore how you're feeling. This is the universe telling you that you're ready for growth.

Don't feel guilty about wanting more. Don't beat yourself up for thinking about all the time that is passing you by and for feeling frustrated by all the opportunities that you're missing out on while you sit behind the desk that you know is not yours.

When thoughts enter your mind and break down your spirit, and you realize you'd be replaced in a heartbeat if you left your job tomorrow, and you wonder why you continue to give your precious time away, stop. Trust that you are in the right place, right here, right now.

When you feel you can't get beyond that little whisper telling you it's time to break free and start your own business, but you are scared as ever to take that next step, stop. Trust you are in the right place, right here, right now.

You're in the place to learn and make the right decisions for you to move forward in the direction that is calling.

The reason it's hard to give yourself permission to make a change is because not very many people do it. It's easier to stay miserable than to walk into the unknown. That is crazy.

Good thing for you…you're different.

CHAPTER 2

Girl, I've Been There, Too

I can tell you, with complete certainty, that you are not crazy.

I have been exactly where you are right now.

I have felt suffocated. I have felt invisible. I have felt ignored and like there is not one more thing that anyone can take from me because I have nothing left to give.

I have felt defeated, ignored, and disrespected.

I can still remember the early days of feeling so excited to go to my job. I was truly thankful to be a leader in a large corporation. I was proud of the opportunity and the impact I believed I was going to make. It's amazing how quickly all that energy was sucked right out of me and my feelings changed.

It's sad, really.

I remember waking up every morning believing I could make a difference. I was confident I would. I looked forward to sharing my knowledge and passion with others and to learning from others. Man, was I excited.

But boy, did that get shut down quickly.

I found myself sitting in meetings surrounded by a bunch of pointless noise. I was surrounded by people who were clueless. People who enjoyed hearing themselves talk and never really took the time to listen to anyone. I could see how this affected my peers. I witnessed, as time went on, less participation and ideas coming out of everyone. Everyone felt like they were defeated before beginning and had no direction. I could see this all around me. It was tough.

I felt like I was in a forever-ongoing game of hot potato, and everyone just wanted to pass the problems around and point fingers. Excuses about *this* not getting done because of *this*, or *that* not getting done because of *that* seemed to be the main agenda of every meeting. I wanted to shout out, "Just stop!" Stop playing this frickin' game, stop wasting time, stop pointing at everyone else, and look at what you can do, look at what I can do, look at what we can do differently. I learned very quickly that that wasn't my place.

My place was to say, okay, I can do that.

I had so many ideas. Ideas to improve productivity at meetings. Ideas to improve connections amongst teammates. Ideas to improve workload and prevent burnout. I went to conferences and seminars outside of the corporation to continue my own learning. No one cared.

For some reason, when I sat in a room of leaders, they seemed to know it all. They all seemed to have the answers, yet no one noticed that we were still talking about the same problems we had been talking about for years.

How was this possible, I wondered? Could no one recognize that if the leader in the room has stopped learning and searching for new ways of doing things, nothing would ever improve?

This wasn't rocket science people, this simply required egos to be crushed.

Before I joined the corporate world, I had owned a business for thirteen years. I started my first business when my first son was one year old. I wanted to be able to care for him myself. I didn't want to send him to daycare or have a babysitter. I wanted to be with him as much as possible, so I designed my business to work around the vision I wanted for my life.

After thirteen years, I made the excruciating choice to close my business. When I say excruciating, I mean it was harder for me to close my business than it was to break my family apart and get divorced. So hard! But several large corporations in the same industry opened around me and I couldn't compete with the big dogs anymore. I had to get real with myself and make the right decision, which just so happened to be the toughest one, too – to close up shop.

So, off into the workforce I went. Talk about scared – it had been about twenty years since I had been in the "workforce." I ended up taking an entry level position I knew I was overqualified for, because I knew I had to start again somewhere. It didn't take me long to get promoted to a leadership position – twelve weeks, in fact. I remember people thinking I was crazy to be going for a promotion so soon. I didn't care though, I went for it and got it. One thing to always remember is that once you gain a new skill, you take it with you wherever you go. All my trainings and certifications served me well at this time. I knew I had the skills to be a good leader. Twelve weeks or not, I was not going to hold myself back.

So, here's the thing about me. I didn't go to college because I didn't want to waste my time sitting in more classrooms being told what to think. Instead I decided to put money into what I knew would give me the greatest return on my investment: myself.

Don't get me wrong, this was very risky, especially in the corporate world, where it seemed college educations were being selected before actual individuals with skills and good character, so a move like not going to college isn't for everyone. But, for me, I knew what I wanted and that was to lead others and not have limits placed on my potential or my income. I also knew I was the only one who could give me what I wanted, so entrepreneurship was the way for me.

I started my journey by reading. I read a lot of books to help me grow and to develop into a better person. I read books on leadership. I read books on getting out of debt and managing money. I read books on entrepreneurship.

I read books on spiritual strengthening. I read books on relationships. I read, read, read.

What I learned though is that it didn't matter how many books I read if I didn't have people challenging and expanding my way of thinking. If I wasn't given a different perspective to look at things, how much was I truly changing as a person, when everything I read was kept at my same level of perspective? I didn't have anyone challenging me to push me, and my thinking, outside of my own box.

I began attending conferences and workshops in cities all around me. I would reserve my seat at any convention offered by the authors of the books I read and loved.

Let me tell you, there is truly no better magic than learning in person. The fairy dust on top of the magic is being surrounded by hundreds of people with a hunger to learn and grow the same as you. The energy in rooms filled with passionate people is contagious, and it's that energy that really catapulted my progress. I already knew I was the only one who could determine my level of success and create my own opportunities, but to have help from others who wanted the same thing was the game changer.

Here's the part that sucks. I hit a brick wall at my corporate job because I didn't have a college degree. Important people wouldn't even look at me when I inquired about higher opportunities. And so, it started…

I began coming home frustrated. I began complaining and whining about all that was waiting for me to do at home. I was angry that my weekends were used for cleaning and laundry and shopping. When was I gonna get a frickin' moment to do something I enjoyed?

One night, it all became clear to me. I had to do something different. My spirit was screaming from within. I remember sitting in my backyard, watching the sunset, feeling completely alone and angry. I remember telling myself I was confused, when really, I knew I wasn't.

I had crystal clarity: I had to do something different. That part I knew.

My confusion seeped in when I thought about what that "something different" was.

I would pray to God in the shower and ask Him to please bring change into my life. To please bring opportunities in my path to do what my heart was craving and give me the wisdom to grab these opportunities when they were in front of me.

Then, He answered, with an opportunity of a lifetime. I found myself in a position to join one of the largest international coaching, speaking and training teams in the world, the John Maxwell Team. If anyone knows anything about leadership, they know who John Maxwell is. We're in over 147 countries, and our coaches and trainers are the best of the best, but I almost missed my opportunity to join.

Here's why I almost missed it: the opportunity didn't look like I thought it would look. It didn't come handed to me with a pretty bow and flashing lights saying, "Here I am, I've been waiting here just for you because you're awesome." In fact, I almost *scrolled* right past it. You read that right, I almost scrolled past one of the opportunities that eventually changed my life, but I didn't. Instead, I "Clicked Here" and my life has never been the same.

It's funny how you can pray for something and the moment you receive a chance to have it, if it doesn't come how you envisioned, you either bypass it, or continue to ask God for a sign. I wonder why we do that. He must shake His head at us all sometimes.

Here's how it went down.

It was a Saturday morning and I wasn't ready to get out of bed. I just didn't want the day to take over yet, so I stayed in bed, grabbed my phone, and got on Facebook. I saw an ad that said something like, "What kind of leader are you?" Oh, you know, I just had to find out.

So, I clicked, took a quiz, got the results. What do you know, I was a great leader who had Entrepreneur DNA. Who comes up with these quizzes?

Whoever came up with the quiz got me to "enter my information in the fields below" and next thing you know, I was on the telephone with someone from the team.

Now, I am one of those people who really doesn't like to be bothered when shopping. If I want it, I'll buy it. If I need help, I'll ask. Otherwise, please just leave me be. But for some reason, when my phone rang, I actually answered it and I had the best conversation with Trent. Suddenly, I had all sorts of information about joining the team, I had excitement in my voice, I had energy pushing me out of bed, and I had thankfulness in my heart. God heard me after all.

Becoming a part of the John Maxwell Team was an honor to me because it was one of John Maxwell's books that I read early on in my development journey that changed my life in that moment. The book was called *Failing Forward*, and that's what I live by now. I fail forward every day.

The bottom line here is, I would never have expected my prayers to be answered by clicking on an ad while scrolling on Facebook from my bed on a Saturday morning attempting to hide from the world. But that's exactly what happened and what my opportunity looked like.

I bet you're wondering right now about the opportunities that maybe you've missed because they didn't come dressed up in bling. It's okay, this could be your bling moment right now.

As part of the John Maxwell Team, I spent months in intense training, both after work and on weekends. I filled myself up with all sorts of new skills and had a completely new outlook on pretty much my whole life. It was A-M-A-Z-I-N-G! The people that were now in my life, the knowledge that was being applied, the perspective that was being shared, and the expansion my mind was going through was exactly what I needed.

All of this from saying yes to myself and taking a chance.

With the prestige from joining this team and learning from one of the best leadership experts in the world, I thought for sure my corporation would see all the opportunity I could bring to us and our employees...but they didn't.

While continuing to do my job every day, I still took the time to have meetings with leaders in other departments at my corporation and explained the programs I felt would benefit our staff on different levels. I had presentations put together to statistically show the benefit some of our programs could offer and how they would even help with employee retention, etc.

The meetings always ended with excitement and the promise of things to come...but they never came.

If there is one thing about having an entrepreneurial mindset that few understand, it is that we don't like to wait. We would rather make a decision and figure out the details while progress is in motion, rather than wait for the right time. We know there is never a right time, instead we know that the time to take action is now.

Get this: I even offered free trainings and workshops to my own peers because I believed so much in the growth and results they would get by working with me, and I knew it would benefit all of us as a team. No one cared. No one wanted to participate. No one had time.

It became very clear that no one wanted to improve, and suddenly, I became very aware of my surroundings.

People wanted answers, but they didn't want to do the work.

I knew I had to develop an exit plan. I could not see myself in the same position, sitting behind the same desk, talking about the same problems with the same people and never seeing improvement. I couldn't do that anymore. It was so hard to work with the John Maxwell Team in the evenings and push excuses and limits out the window, and then go to work in the mornings and be surrounded by excuses and limits. No, I had to develop a way out.

So, it began. *If they won't let me utilize my skills of coaching, speaking, and training, I will utilize them myself.* The sad part was, I loved my team. I didn't want to leave them, but I knew I couldn't serve them well either if no one was going to give me an opportunity to do more. A cap had been placed on my potential at my job, and I knew I would not serve my team well because I was no longer in alignment with what I valued the most: growth and continually becoming more while doing better.

Know yourself, know your potential, and create your own opportunities if no one is going to give you any!

Enter…the start of a new business.

I worked on my business for a year while still at my job. I don't want to mislead you. I didn't wake up one morning and think, I hate my job, so I think I'll quit today and tomorrow I'll open for business.

No, I worked hard for a year, developing my business while going to my job. The way I looked at it, my job was my silent investor. The money I made from my job contributed to the start-up of my company.

So, believe me when I say it is quite possible to start a business even when you think you have nothing to start it with. You must be smart and strategic about it, though. Put the money in the places that are going to matter most.

Most often, because we see things from the outside looking in, it's common to put money into the things that really don't matter. Don't make those types of mistakes (no worries, I'll share what those are in a bit).

So, with my plan in place, I gave my four months' notice and felt good about it. It was a clean decision.

It takes a lot of internal searching to know that change is required to stay true to your values and your spirit.

It takes courage to step into what you know is right for you, especially when, from the outside, others don't understand your choices.

I had to remind myself often that my journey was not about what others thought. Others weren't giving me their minutes of life. No, mine were being used up doing something I didn't love, and I would not get them back.

I do understand the journey of becoming more and more frustrated when it comes to the monotonous routine of going to a dead-end job every day. I lived it for four years.

I do not regret any part of it because it taught me so much. It also gave me the wisdom required to move forward and walk in faith, and I am so happy I did, because it has brought me here to you.

If I was stuck and still sitting behind the desk that was "not my desk," you would not be reading this book right now.

I would not be able to help you on your journey of understanding that you do have what it takes to do whatever it is your heart is craving.

I have made mistakes and I have had huge success. I have owned businesses and I have closed businesses. I have worked for others and others have worked for me. I have hired people and I have fired people. I have asked questions and I have given answers. All of it has been done from my heart, because I genuinely want the best for others.

You have a unique gift and it's wrapped in what's called opportunity.

That something deep inside of you screaming to get out is making its way. I know, because, girl, I've been there, too.

CHAPTER 3

You Already Have What It Takes

I remember what it feels like to waste time at a job that isn't bad, but just isn't the job for you. I also remember the guilt that comes along with those feelings. I want different for you.

It's not that you're ungrateful, it's that you have so much inside that you want to share, and you can't. It sucks. Not to mention how much it plays with your mind.

You begin to believe that staying stuck is your only option. You begin to believe that it's wrong of you to want more because you're doing alright right now. Am I right?

It's hard because the more you change, the further away from others you grow. It's a lonely place to be. It's like you're standing in the middle of a crowd of people, yet everyone is so far away.

The thing is, time can't be replaced, just as you can't be replaced.

But, somehow, the workforce reminds you daily of how replaceable you really are.

So, I ask you, why be so hesitant to make a move? Why give up more time that you will never get back? Why put yourself on hold while everyone else moves on?

It's time to believe in yourself, embrace your uniqueness, and do what your spirit is calling. You do have what it takes, so stop wasting your time and let the Broken Stronger Boss Lady inside of you make her debut.

I'm gonna go deep here and share with you one of the strongest forces that motivated me to make the bold changes I knew I had to make: my children.

When I'd lay in bed at night, knowing there was more to me than I was sharing with the world, I would think of my boys. I could not imagine them growing up, watching me spend each day full of frustration. I didn't want them to see me without a smile every evening. I didn't want them to see me grouchy and tired all the time. They deserved better from me. I wanted to be an example to them that would alter their life, in a good way. It was up to me to show them what it looked like to work hard for something you want.

They needed to know, early on, that they had options and limitless potential. It was my responsibility to let them know, and show them, that if they had dreams and their hearts desired something unique and amazing, they could have it.

I didn't want to corrupt their minds by making them believe life was meant only for clocking in and out and working for someone else. That it was okay to be drained of precious time and energy daily. And I for sure didn't want to show them that it was okay for a cap or limit to be placed on their financial success. No way. I had to show them that type of power did not fall under the authority of someone else.

No, I had a huge responsibility to show my boys that they could have anything they wanted if they were willing to work for it.

They were my driving force and motivation when I felt like giving up a time or two. Everyone goes through those moments of wondering if this is the right path, or if the risk is worth it, and the answer is, yes, it is. You are worth it. Your legacy is worth it.

I know you may feel stuck and paralyzed to move forward. I did too. I sometimes felt like I had no options and no one on my side. I felt very alone.

However, I'll let you in on a few discoveries I've made along the way. You are not stuck. You simply must let go of a current part of you to make room for a different version of you. The true version of you.

You are not paralyzed either. You just don't know what step to take next. That is okay. Feeling paralyzed and not knowing what to do next is normal. The fact that you can acknowledge this feeling is something you should be proud of because it's a unique indicator, given directly to you, letting you know you are meant for more.

I know right now it feels like you are alone. My friend, believe me, you are not, and the good thing is you do have options. You don't have to stay in this situation for the rest of your life.

Let's start some movement forward right now by looking at a few things head on, shall we:

- You know your situation at your job will not change. It hasn't after all this time. Even though you have good days, the bad days win.

- You feel suffocated. You're ready for growth and new challenges and they aren't being provided.

- You have thoughts floating around in your head that scare you, and it seems impossible to you right now to start a business. Rightly so, you haven't done it yet. Or maybe you have, and it didn't work out. You just didn't have the right people in place to help you along.

I want to share a little secret with you. When you learn how to make fear and doubt work in your favor, consider yourself virtually unstoppable.

This is one of the many things I will share with you in my process, called The Mariposa Effect.

In case you didn't know, "mariposa" is butterfly in Spanish. So, I'm sure you've heard of the butterfly effect: change one thing, change everything. That is the basis behind my process, because it begins with just one thing – and that one thing is you.

I chose the butterfly because it's a representation of the transformation we all go through from feeling suffocated in a cocoon to breaking free and flying high.

The truth is, anytime something new is about to take place in life, fear and doubt begin to flow in because they like to hang out with the unknown.

The feelings you have right now are completely normal. I don't think it would be normal to start anything brand new without some feelings of hesitance, fear, and doubt. I mean, it is the unknown after all. Of course it's scary.

However, when you learn how to combine determination and confidence with action, you will achieve a level of success that right now you can't fathom. A level of success that others don't understand and think you're crazy for wanting.

There are no shortcuts to success. If it were easy, everyone would do it. There is, however, a priority to the order of doing things, and this is where most get tripped up.

It's taken me years to figure out this journey, and the reason I have put The Mariposa Effect together is to be for you what I needed years ago. I wish I had known someone who could have guided me along the way, instead of having to learn by trial and error.

That's not to say that there won't be mistakes along the way. We all have to learn from our own mistakes, but what I have found over the years is that there is a common order to things in order for success to happen, and that is what I want to share with you in my process.

So, if you feel like you're that beautiful mariposa stuck in her suffocating cocoon, here's what is ahead for you.

The first thing I'm going to ask you is to stop window shopping. I am going to ask you to stop simply wishing and wanting for things to get different because every time you do, you are pushing your dream further away from you.

Think about it. What good does it do to walk around the shopping mall just looking through the windows at all the things you wish you could have or drooling over all the things you want? That is a waste of time and makes you feel depressed because you hate that you work all the time and still can't have what you want. It puts you on an insecurity trip because you wonder how everyone else can go in and buy whatever they want. And if you do buy what you want, knowing darn well you shouldn't, you end up feeling guilty or stressed afterward – and where is the joy in that?

No, my friend, window shopping is a spiral down into the black hole of pity and before you know it, instead of not being able to have just one thing, you feel like your whole life sucks.

Window shopping brings nothing into your possession. It is pointless and a waste. Therefore, I am going to teach you right away the difference between wishing and wanting vs. actually attaining the things your heart desires. I'm going to teach you how to go in and get it!

Then, I'm going to give you ways to remove all the noise, aka *doubt, fear,* and *insecurity* that surround you and shut out the amazing ideas in your head.

Do you remember, back in the day, when you'd turn the dial on a radio station and catch a glimpse of a song you loved in between all the static? Don't judge me, I know I'm totally showing my age here. Anyway, you kept turning the dial until you could hear your jam. No more static.

With several of my techniques, it's the same thing. You will be able to receive clarity, instead of confusion. Most importantly, you'll learn to trust and act on the very ideas in your own head, instead of hiding them or shutting them down before you even give them a chance.

The ideas in your mind are given to you because you're meant to do something with them. You might think they are too great for someone like you. Newsflash, you are that great.

Which brings me to another thing we'll cover in my process: your strength. This is one of the things so often missed, overlooked, and ignored, because you don't see it. You're too close. Amazing things happen when you can see your own strength.

Get ready to stand in front of a mirror, beautiful, because you will soon be revealing your own strength. The most important person to convince of your power is the one staring back at you. Once you believe in her, hang on, because she's going to take you places.

You're finally going to look fear in the face and tell it to go to h-e-double hockey sticks. Yes, fear is real, but your strength is strong, and when you become the Broken Stronger Boss that you were born to be, you'll become unstoppable.

Lastly, one of the most important pieces I'll mention here, so that we can get right into all the good stuff in this book, is learning how to design your future. Yes, this is a thing and I'll show you how to begin. It might sound near impossible to do, but if it were impossible, you wouldn't be reading my book right now – the book I was able to write after I left my job.

You, too, can learn to design your future, and if you are not sure you can, that's even more reason for you to keep right on reading, girl, and learn how.

The bottom line is, whatever your dream looks like, you can breathe life into it – and I can show you how.

It really all boils down to honoring your ideas, putting them into action, working smart, and getting results. Therefore, I don't want you to wait another minute to get started.

I want you to be able to see what is working – and what isn't working – quickly, because your time is that valuable and shouldn't be wasted.

I know it's hard to imagine right now how different your life can be, but I want you to know that it can be different.

With a few steps that are often overlooked, steps that I can teach you, you can change the design of your future.

Entrepreneurship is not for everyone, but you owe it to yourself to find out if it's right for you.

Broken Stronger Boss reality check: if you're not willing to sacrifice a few weeks to be able to make a clean yes or no decision, then this isn't the right path for you. Save yourself some time and money, put the book down now, and learn to get comfortable in doing what you've always done.

However, if you are willing to invest in yourself and give it all you've got for a few short weeks, then the opportunities ahead of you are limitless. The odds of winning are determined only by the bets you're willing to place on yourself.

Your determination plus your action. Now, that's a winning combination right there!

CHAPTER 4

Stop Wishing Already

THE MARIPOSA EFFECT
M – Magnify Your Desire

Y ou must desire in order to receive. This may sound either completely off the wall to you, or extremely simple, but the truth is, it's complicated but required in becoming your own boss.

I hate to break it to you, but there are no cookie cutter steps to success. I wish there were, but then it would be easy for everyone, and what you're about to do isn't for everyone. In fact, since no two people are the same, no two things work exactly the same for each of us. However, there are several critical components that anyone who has ever achieved success agree upon, and in this step, we'll cover the very first one.

I want you to begin by answering this question: What do you desire?

Note, I did not ask, "What do you want?" "What do you wish for?" I asked, "What do you desire?"

What's the difference between a desire vs. a want or wish, you ask? Girl, I'll tell you the difference. One you will have, the other you will never have. Ouch!

The bonus for you right now is that most people never think about this question, let alone answer it, so you're already a step ahead. And because you're a Broken Stronger Boss and are different, that is why you are going to have the success that others do not.

Before you quickly answer this question, let's talk about the difference between wanting and wishing for something vs. having a desire for it.

This is the point where I want you to envision yourself window shopping. The thing sitting behind the window you're staring at is your dream, your passion, your goal, your success.

When you're in the mind space of wanting or wishing for something, you stay in the state of want and wish. This means your dream will always be out of reach, it will always be behind the window. You'll spend all the days of your life, forever wanting and wishing, always walking by and always being able to peek at it, because in want and wish state, that's where it will forever remain.

Desire, on the other hand, is actively participating in the attainment of your goal. In other words, when you desire something, you're already in the state of bringing it to you. Your dream, your passion, your goal, your success is in motion, it's active, it's on its way to you because you're reaching for it.

Desire is choosing to walk into the store without knowing how you're going to get what's behind the window but trusting that, once in the store, you will do what it takes to be sure you don't leave without it. Legally, of course.

So, let me ask you now, where are you when it comes to the idea of starting your business?

Are you spending your time wanting and wishing for a business, or are you actively seeking the ways in which you can bring your business to life?

Putting this very first step under the magnifying glass will give you clarity that you can act upon.

Clarity required to begin the journey forward.

In fact, taking time to complete this step alone will set you apart from the amateurs who spend more time talking about all they want and all they wish for, but will never have. Prepare yourself now, because you'll begin to see things differently right away, and once you are in the true state of desire, everyone will need to stand back and make way because you'll be on the move. Or (how I like to refer to it), you'll be on a mission – and my mantra is "I'm on a mission, consider it done."

As adults, it's easy to kill off the idea of a dream. It's easy to tell ourselves that it is silly or stupid to have a dream because that is what we've been programmed to believe. Dreams don't come true. Dreams are for people who keep their heads in the clouds. Dreams are for "those" people. Most times, this programming comes from our own parents. God love them, but they can be dream killers.

I was fortunate to grow up with parents who were entrepreneurs. At one point, I believe they owned seven businesses. I learned very early on the power of desire and what it looks like when it's in motion. I always knew that I could do whatever I set my mind to, but I can't say that my ideas were always supported.

I remember being in grade school, seventh grade in fact, and the questions that started popping up from my guidance counselors about what college I wanted to go to. They wanted to know what I was going to major in, what type of college degree would work best for me. They even had me take tests to see what careers I'd be most compatible with. I remember telling them, "I am going to be a cartoonist at Walt Disney," and my plan was to go the Art Institute. I mean, come on, in seventh grade who doesn't want to work at Disney? It was my dream job. That wasn't a very popular answer, or plan, amongst my guidance counselors.

So, for me, it was my guidance counselors who started putting doubt in my dream. For others, it's their parents.

I mean, how often do parents (or adults with influence, like guidance counselors) suggest you look within to determine if you have a hidden desire lying dormant? Not very often.

No, they most likely suggested safe careers that would provide security. That's okay, they just wanted the best for you, and it may have been the only way they knew.

Most times when you see an adult making a career move, it's because they spent most of their adult life living someone else's dream and are done with it.

I have seen so many successful adults leave great corporate, high paying jobs to start small businesses. I've seen podiatrists leave to start designing shoes, I've seen lawyers leave to start cupcake businesses. It really doesn't matter what you've done before, what matters is what you do moving forward.

You have a gift, a purpose that you're not living right now That is why you are here. You are working to bring someone else's dream to life, and you're tired of it. It's alright to feel this way, and it's alright to do something about it. That talent that belongs to you and no one else, the one you still question, the one you're hiding from the world, is fighting to get out, and rightly so. You are one-of-a-kind, so why should you be doing what can be done by a million other people? Do what you were created to do. And so, I ask you again – what do you desire?

Where do you fall on the scale of wanting and wishing for something or truly desiring it with all your being?

Let me share something with you. You can start a business, if that is what you desire. It is possible.

Is it going to be easy? No. Is it going to make you money right away? No. Is it going to require hard work, effort, sweat, and sometimes tears? Yes.

This is the reason it is imperative to start with this one important question. Do you desire to have your own business? Do you desire it so badly you can taste it? Do you desire it so badly, you don't care how many opinions come your way saying you're crazy for doing so? Because that will happen.

As you focus on this step, think about the real reason behind your desire to start your own business.

The most common reason is autonomy. You don't want anyone telling you what to do and when to do it. You don't want anyone putting a cap on your potential or the amount of money you can make. You don't want someone dictating how you spend your time, and you surely don't want to work every single day of your year, only to have to ask permission to have one week off and hope that you get it.

No, you want to be your own boss, call the shots, pay yourself, take the time off when you want, take vacations, and be the Broken Stronger Boss that you know you are.

I have another question for you. Warning, I have a lot of questions for you along the way.

Behind your desire to start a business, do you plan to be a business owner or an entrepreneur? Whoa, what's the difference you ask? There is a big difference.

Most people around you are business owners. Meaning, they have taken the concept of working for someone else and just applied it to themselves. They are now clocking in and out for themselves and end up working longer hours for less pay.

Enter the reason most people think you're nuts for starting a business of your own. It's what they normally see, so who can blame them?

However, if you start your business with an entrepreneurial mindset, you will set your business up to generate income even while you sleep, or while on vacation, or while taking a day off. This is very different from simply being a business owner.

Do yourself a favor and determine the answers to these questions before anything else. What do you desire? Do you plan to be a business owner or an entrepreneur?

The saying goes *"jump and build your wings on the way down."* This is true in some cases, but not in all cases.

Knowing the right time to jump is going to make a huge impact on your level of success. There are times you must jump and push through your fear to make progress. There are other times you must make progress before you jump.

Therefore, be sure you are learning from the right type of mentor, surrounding yourself with the people who will ask you the right types of questions based on your desire.

If you go around jumping here and there, without a parachute, you will quickly realize that you're in one big free fall and don't even have a landing pad in place. Don't do that. That's not what a Broken Stronger Boss does.

So, in the step Magnify Your Desire, gauge where you currently are on the scale of want and wish vs. desire. This is critical.

Once you are confident you have arrived at the state of desire, ask yourself if you want to be a business owner or an entrepreneur, then get moving. Put the right people in place to help you along your path by finding people who have what you want and doing what they do.

What will make your business unique and different is you. Don't ever get caught up in the game of comparison, especially when just starting out.

It's not about what others think. It's not about pride and ego. It's about knowing you have gifts to share with the world and that someone needs you. So, I ask you, what is one thing you can do today to begin actively participating in the design of your future, your dream, your business?

When you find yourself believing you don't have what it takes to start your own business, which you will, remember this…this is false! You do have what it takes.

In fact, you are already one step ahead because you are reading this book, and I have you starting with one of the most important details that many fail to ask themselves… do you want and wish, or do you desire?

Desire will keep you moving forward when you feel like quitting.

Desire will shut out the voices of opinion that will surely be offered your way.

Desire will open doors of opportunity for you.

Desire will turn your dream into reality.

Desire will be the guiding force to keep you on your path when starting your business.

When you are passionate about something, it doesn't go away. This is the beauty of pairing desire with passion. You will become unstoppable the moment you recognize that both are imperative to success.

If you have a true passion within your spirit and a desire to bring it to life...watch out world, here she comes!

I'm gonna let you in on another valuable piece of information that will blow your mind.

Ninety-eight percent of the people out there want and wish for something different. Two percent of the people out there desire something different and do the work required. Two percent won't tolerate mediocrity when it comes to making their own dreams come true. Be a two percenter!

The dreams inside of you do not belong to anyone else. No one will understand why you want to go on this journey. It's not for them to understand. You don't need their permission to live your dream.

I caution you now, you will find yourself not wanting to be surrounded by wanters and wishers. It will drive you nuts. You'll want to surround yourself with doers and achievers. People who desire to be different and are actively participating in making change happen.

If you are struggling with not knowing if you truly desire to start your own business and think it may still be a want or a wish, don't worry. This doesn't mean you will never have your own business, it simply means you have a little more digging to do within. It means you are not ready now.

However, be sure you're not confusing lack of desire with worry about not knowing how you're going to do it. We're not there yet. I will help you when the time comes, but we can't determine how to get there if we don't even know where there is.

Now is not the time to come out of the gates as though you already have all the answers. There will come a day when you are able to help someone else on this journey from the other side; however, for now, take this opportunity to learn all you can. You will move forward to success much faster and with a higher climb.

Be proud of yourself. You are changing the path of your future and your family's future and showing what it means to take dreams from hanging out in the clouds amongst the rainbows and fairy dust and pulling them into your grasp so they can be lived each day.

You will have a new energy, a new joy in your life, because you will be doing what your heart's purpose desires.

You will be living in your sweet spot, and your creative energy and laughter will surface. People will be exposed to the real you, the genuine you, the you that the world so desperately needs.

Don't feel you can't let your uniqueness be celebrated. Do that thing that your heart is asking you to do and honor who God created you to be. There is absolutely nothing wrong with standing tall and proud of who you are and sharing your voice with the world.

Be you!

So, it's time to take out your magnifying glass and place under it the question, "Do you want and wish for different or do you desire for different?" What is your answer?

To achieve success and have a functioning and profitable business, you must desire it. You can't want or wish for it to just fall into your lap.

The choice is yours and the power is yours. You have what it takes to make it happen. Now, go get it!

CHAPTER 5

That Little Voice in Your Head Is Real

THE MARIPOSA EFFECT
A – Acknowledge Your Inner Voice

Now that you know what it is you desire, it's time to pay attention to what the little voice inside your head is telling you.

I know she talks to you. What is she saying?

Is she telling you that your dream is too big? Is she telling you that you're nuts for thinking you can start a business and leave your job? Is she telling you that you must be out of your mind if you think you can be successful and have all you envision? Is she telling you that success like that is for "them," and no way do you have what it takes to make your life that successful?

This is where you need to determine which voice you're going to listen to – the little voice that seems to never stop doubting and tells you you can't, or the bigger voice of wisdom that knows the truth and tells you you can.

One of the biggest components to success is one that is not talked about often, but that will make all the difference in the type of success you attract and receive.

What is this unspoken component? Faith.

Yes, faith.

I don't know what you call it, and I don't need to know what you call it, but it's a belief in a higher energy, a bigger power, a faith in something bigger than yourself. Some call it Master of the Universe, others call it Love. I like to call it my G.O.D., My Grand Overall Designer.

My G.O.D. is that something bigger than myself that connects us all together and is the one component of success that determines how high we can go.

It is through high levels of faith that your inner voice grows louder, clearer, and speaks with confidence and authority – aka, discernment.

Without a high level of discernment, the best of leaders can bring down a great team in record time, and businesses with the potential for great success can crumble rapidly or never get off the ground.

Discernment is the secret sauce that will lift you up and hold you on a high level all your own. The more in tune you become with the voice of wisdom from within, the more people will take notice and begin to listen to you.

When people of high discernment speak, people listen. They speak with a calmness, a confidence, and an authority.

They don't use so many noisy and meaningless words. They don't need to.

I'm sure you can tell when you're around someone who speaks from this internal voice as opposed to those that just speak to hear their own voice. There is a shallowness and a constant movement of nothing important that comes from people who just want to hear their own voice as opposed to a depth and purposefulness that comes from people that speak with confidence and wisdom within.

The question to ask yourself in this step is where do you stand on your own level of discernment and in trusting that your own internal voice is coming from a higher source?

When it comes to business, this voice is important.

It is the voice of clarity that will assist you in making decisions. You will be faced with making many decisions on a regular basis, and this wisdom will guide you to know you are making the right decisions and for the right reasons.

Some of the most successful people, when asked, will tell you there is a higher source they go to for guidance and wisdom.

This isn't one of those things that is published in magazine articles and posted on social media (unless faith is a topic), but let's be honest, how often do you see that type of stuff talked about? Not very often.

Truth is, the most successful people, the people who make the most impact and have a high level of influence and respect, are those with a high knowing of self.

When you take inventory of the people who have made the most impact to you and have held a high level of influence over your life, they probably have a sense of calmness about them. They probably emit a sense of caring, a gentle authority, and are full of encouragement and belief in you. You feel cared for by these types of people.

As you continue your journey of starting your business, it's important to determine right up front what type of leader you want to be. Think about what you want to be known for and how you want people to perceive you. Think about the type of people you want to do business with and, when the time comes to make important decisions, think about how you'll know you're making the right ones for you.

Yes, this is a lot to think about, but it's the name of the game. You will be faced with having to make decisions all the time. One of the greatest assets you can invest in is yourself and the development of higher discernment. This will enable you to go within for the answers you will continually seek and trust the voice that speaks to you.

I'll be honest, this is a tough topic and one that requires confidence. I am able to share the importance of developing discernment because it's the only reason you're reading this book.

Let me explain.

In February 2018, I was laid up at home because I had had a very serious neck surgery and had nothing but time on my hands. I was in the process of creating training material for one of the workshops I offer and my G.O.D. told me I was going to write a book. Now, I know what His voice sounds like because my discernment is very strong. It's something that I can say is a gift of mine, and that I have placed intentional focus on finetuning for years. So, when I heard the command to write a book, I knew exactly what it was…I just didn't want to believe it.

That was honestly a time I told God, "I think you made a mistake. I am not a writer." Seriously, I told Him that. Have you ever told God He's made a mistake? I'm sure I made Him chuckle.

For over five days, the idea, the thought, the voice, all of it kept repeating in my head: you're going to write a book, you're going to write a book, you're going to write a book. It would not stop. I didn't tell anyone, I just laid in my recliner, healing my neck, listening to this crazy idea in my head. This crazy idea that I still didn't believe.

On February 6, 2018, it all changed. It was bedtime and I was brushing my teeth. While toothpaste ran down my arm (hey, doesn't that happen to everyone?) I was still thinking about the crazy idea of writing a book…really, thinking it was nuts and could leave my mind at any time.

Then, loud and clear, I heard *"You will write a book. It will be called 'Broken Stronger.'"* Boom! Just like that. What the heck was that? I knew what it was – it was God tired of me doubting His command for over five days. He decided to put a stop to my doubt and told me exactly what was gonna happen.

What happened next was even more crazy than the idea of writing. God flashed before me, like a movie trailer, all my life's pains. Like, pain clear back from when I was a little girl, all of it. I saw them all like screenshots just flipping from one to the next and to the next.

In an instant, I was bawling. Yes, bawling with toothpaste all over me.

I was crying because God let me see how strong I was. He let me see all that I had been through. He also let me know this was the reason He was calling on me to write this book. He did not put me through all that pain throughout my life for no reason. No, He had been conditioning me, my whole life, for this very moment. He had been giving me the lessons and the wisdom and the faith to be able to carry out His plan and help you.

Then He scooped up all my pain and He took it away. God can do that, you know. He took it away, because He was making room for other things. Things I will share with you later, but the bottom line is, when God talks, you listen.

In the bathroom, after what felt like hours (but was only minutes), I said out loud back to God, "Okay, I trust you. I will write this book and I trust you will give me the words."

Before I went to bed that night, I had researched the book name to make sure it wasn't taken (of course it wasn't, God gave it to me) and put the plan in motion. I didn't worry about the details, because I knew they would come. I had the important parts down, I had a burning desire to complete my task, and I had trust in the voice that was telling me, "I can and I will," two of the most powerful components to success.

That's the power of discernment and why it's important for you and for your success.

Not many people think of discernment as a skill, and therefore they never work on developing it, but it can change everything. That's what I'm about and what my process is about, remember? Change one thing…change everything. Discernment is one thing that can truly change everything, so let's work on this skill now.

I know you have that voice inside that speaks to you. I know you do, and it's the voice that has been telling you that you are done wasting your time, that you are meant for more, that you have gifts to share with the world, and that you are ready to start your business. It's that voice that told you to buy this book. It's the voice that assures you that you have what it takes. So, yes, you have that voice that speaks to you. We all do.

However, do you trust this voice? Do you believe in the things it tells you?

Does the voice come in fuzzy or does it come in loud and clear?

There are several ways to bring clarity to your inner voice.

One of them is to spend time alone, in silence, focused on the question at hand and the decisions that need to be made.

I know, it's hard to just sit in silence and listen. It's hard to push all the noise of the world out and just sit…still…quiet.

You'll be amazed at the thoughts, ideas, answers, and clarity that come to you when you take a moment to shush the noise around you, though. Before you take this time alone, state in your mind, say out loud, or write down (it doesn't matter how) the question(s) you're confused about. Put them out there, and then listen in solitude.

Don't ignore all the things that come to you when you take this moment to be alone and quiet. Give yourself that time and then write down what comes to you. Write it down because you will forget.

Another approach is to talk with a mentor or coach, someone you greatly respect and admire. Explain to them the decisions you're struggling with making and talk it through. God will speak to you through other people.

When choosing these people to reach out to, determine why them. Ask yourself, what is it about them that you admire and respect? Think about talking with successful businesspeople who you aspire to be like. Choose people who are well put together and confident. When these people come to mind, ask yourself what about them draws you to want to know more from them. Put care and effort in when picking these people, because any time you ask someone for an opinion, it should be someone you're willing to trade places with. They will share with you what they know, and what they know has given them results. Be sure you pay attention to their results.

In other words, do not ask your broke Uncle Chuck, who spends more time on his couch than anywhere else, what you should do or what he thinks about you starting a successful business. I don't care how much you love him or how much ice cream he bought you when you were little.

The advice he will give you, the place he will speak from, is the information that has made him broke and has him spending his time on the couch.

Get what I'm saying here?

Don't go to your parents and ask them for advice on starting a successful business if they are living each of their days going to a dead-end job and their dream was to have a long-lasting marriage.

Again, they will only be able to give you advice from the place they know.

They may be happy, they may have a good solid marriage, but they are not the best candidates to give you good business advice. Most likely, they will encourage you to stay put in your job and tell you you're lonely and just need to find a good man and settle down.

Who you choose to receive advice and help from is a huge component in your success when on your business journey.

So, that brings me to another person you should stay away from, even though she will be the first one you want to go to: don't go to your best girlfriend either. If she isn't living it herself, what can she possibly tell you about doing it yourself? Not a frickin' thing, but believe me, she'll think she's an expert and you'll walk away from wine night more messed up in the head than ever before.

Choose wisely!

Another thing you can do to gain clarity and wisdom is to simply determine when you're going to focus on it. You'll learn very quickly on this journey that you don't just "find" time and you don't just "get" time, you must assign time.

Don't wander around aimlessly, telling yourself that when you find the time, you'll sit and think about this stuff and try to come up with the answers you're seeking.

No, designate and assign the time when you will actively work on seeking answers.

Consider things like, when do you find it easier to be alone (morning/afternoon/evening) and the number of days per week you want to make this a focus. Be honest with yourself and then put it on your calendar.

Don't leave these appointments with your G.O.D. and the conversations with your inner voice to chance or until you see how your week unfolds. There is a common element to successful people when it comes to delegating their time: they schedule time for things that are a priority and non-negotiable. They don't leave it to chance.

So, pick the day(s) of the week and the time of day, and block off a chunk in your calendar to intentionally focus on the questions that need answered.

Then keep your appointment. You wouldn't cancel a hair appointment or a doctor's appointment just because you don't have time; don't cancel this one either. It's probably one of the most important appointments you can make for your success because the answers are always within you and the voice inside that talks to you knows best.

Business is all about making decisions. Decisions that ultimately attract your desired outcome. And developing wisdom is the best way to discover answers to the decisions that need to be made. It's a powerful circle. Therefore, one of the most important investments you can make in yourself and one that few ever focus on is the development of wisdom, discernment, and ultimately faith. Faith in your G.O.D., faith in yourself, faith in your abilities and in your potential. It will not only serve you well in the growth of your business, but in your life, and will be a huge factor in the type of Broken Stronger Boss you become.

Since it's rarely talked about, I don't know if people are afraid to say that they have a foundation of faith when it comes to business, but, to me, it sure is more comforting to know I'm working with someone who is going to a higher source when looking for wisdom and answers than claiming they know it all on their own and have shut their brains off to anything higher than themselves. No thank you. I will work with someone else.

Here's the thing: I am confident in the role faith plays in success (and intrigued by the fact that faith is not discussed more) that I became curious about what others thought, so I asked many of my powerful and strong woman leader peers to answer a questionnaire for me. One of the questions I asked was whether they believed faith played a role in their success. With a 100% response rate, the answer was a clear "yes." Something to think about…

The choice is entirely up to you and how you choose to move forward when it comes to strengthening your gift of discernment. However, there are some things I find to be true.

Listen to your voice inside and believe it when it tells you, "You can." Believe it when it gives you an idea and wants you to turn that idea into something concrete.

Believe your voice inside when it tells you that you can have more, do better, and break free to take your time back.

Believe your voice inside when it tells you what your next step is. Maybe you can't see beyond that very next step, but you don't need to.

Any journey can only be taken one step at a time, and this includes the journey of starting your business.

I am so passionate about you developing this step. Here are a few more ideas on how to receive answers to your questions and gain trust and wisdom from the voice within.

Lay the question(s) directly in front of you and list the facts you already have. You may be surprised at how much you already know.

Look for answers all around you. Messages and ideas come from all over the place. They may be in a song you hear while driving, in a movie you watch with your kids, in a conversation you have with people you care about, or in this book as you read right now.

Messages and answers come to you all the time from all around. It's your awareness and willingness to look for them that will make all the difference.

Listen to your thoughts. Once an idea comes into your mind it is an idea for a second time. You didn't create it. You didn't invent something brand new. God had the idea first and He chose you to give it to.

Think about how many ideas are given to people every day and nothing ever becomes of them. It's sad, think about it. All these dreams that are floating around being given to people who never bring them to life.

Do not ever give your dream a chance to come to your bedside when your time on earth is done and ask why you never paid attention to it. Don't ever let it tell you, "I came to you. I wanted you to do something with me. Why did you ignore me? Why didn't you ever bring me to life?" Yeah, don't ever let your dream be able to ask you those questions.

You have what it takes to make your dreams come true. You have desire, you have wisdom, and you have me on your side, cheering you along.

You are not meant to live small. You are not designed to just take up space and breathe in air and not live your dream.

Make your time count. Live the life you desire. Listen to your voice inside. Make yourself a priority and share your awesomeness. You have it inside. You do.

CHAPTER 6

Time to Strip it Down

THE MARIPOSA EFFECT
R – Reveal Your Strength

So, here's the thing. You've stopped wishing and wanting, because you know Broken Stronger Bosses don't wish and want, we desire! You've started listening and trusting your inner voice and know it's full of wisdom. Wisdom that will drive you toward success. You've shut down that little voice of doubt that keeps messing with you and playing tug of war in your head.

Now, I want to ask: what do you still have going on inside of you that makes you believe starting a business and being successful is for "them" and not for you? Because I know it's still there, and I bet it has something to do with the programming you've been faced with all your life.

Programming that has come from parents telling you "no" and punishing you for every mistake you've made. Programming from algebra teachers treating you differently because you failed a test. Programming from PE teachers failing you for not being able to jump hurdles (okay, that one's mine).

Programming sucks, and we have all been programmed.

If you don't believe we have all been programmed, do a little exercise with me, right now. Finish these sentences:

The early bird catches the _ _ _ _.

Good things come to those who _ _ _ _.

Money doesn't grow on _ _ _ _ _.

I'm sure you could finish those sentences, and we have never met in person. I didn't teach them to you, and I don't remember who taught them to me. This was an exercise we did in a training seminar with over three thousand people from around the globe. Each of us could finish the sentences, yet none of us grew up together. If that isn't programming, I don't know what is.

So, whatever the reason you think you don't have what it takes to break free and start your own business, realize this thought is false. This thinking is probably coming from some programming that needs to be undone.

I want you to take a moment to stop and take a look backwards at all the things you've done, things you've accomplished, things that at one point you thought you'd never be able to do.

Be honest here. Now is not the time to be modest; you know these moments exist. Please don't tell yourself that you haven't really done anything that great. You have.

Now I want you to think of some of the things that scared the crap out of you at one point that you didn't think you'd get through. You got through them, right?

You either succeeded or you failed. It doesn't matter, you got through them, and you're still alive and well to think about them, right?

My point is, you have gotten through some of the hardest times of your life, when at one point you didn't think you'd be able to, and you probably did it without a thought-out plan, clear strategy, or help along the way. You know why? You have what it takes. You're a Broken Stronger Boss…that is why.

Imagine what you can do when you put intentional focus around breaking free from the confinement of a job you hate and commit to stop wasting your precious time. Imagine what you can do when you accept that it is okay to dream big and succeed. Wow, just imagine.

We've already established that starting a business is not for everyone, even though the reasons for wanting to be your own boss are sometimes universal, like time freedom, financial freedom, and limitless opportunities, etc. But here's something I want you to consider (and be honest with yourself) – does your ego have anything to do with it?

If you want the title, authority, and recognition and think being a business owner is going to immediately give you respect or make you a step above others, that, my friend, is ego, and that does not bring success.

So, if you feel Mr. Ego is making his debut and peeking his head around the corner, telling you, "Hey, you know I'm coming with you on this journey, right?" It's time to let him know right away that he is not welcome to join, nor invited to your party.

Many times, people don't think about this in advance and end up realizing much too late that their ego joined in the journey right from the beginning.

You may be wondering what effects ego can have on the success of your business. There are several.

Ego will quickly stop you in your tracks because it doesn't like to do the hard work required and thinks it's too good for certain things. It will tell you that you don't really have to do that tedious work because you're the boss and it's beneath you.

Ego likes pride and to do things on its own, and suddenly, you'll find yourself standing all alone with only ego to keep you company. You don't have a business if you don't have people around you. No one will want to hear from you. No one will want to work with you. It will be extremely hard to grow your business if ego is present.

Ego likes to be the expert and know it all, so it rarely takes chances and tries new things. It doesn't want to be seen making a mistake. So, if ego is present, you will not learn, you will not grow, you will not be creative and innovative, all things required to grow a successful business.

I encourage you to take the time to really think about this now. Why do you want to start your own business? If there is more of a pride and entitlement vibe flowing with you on this one, we need to quickly determine why and crush it.

The bottom line is, when starting your business, you will have to start at the bottom.

That is truth right there, and I am not one to sugarcoat things nor dress hard work in pretty rainbows and ribbons. No. You will have to start at the bottom and do work. There are no shortcuts to creating a business that steadily grows and works for you. So, if someone is trying to feed you some bull crap instant business success magic pill… run, Forrest, run!

I bring this up because I've seen a lot of dreams die, simply because people thought reaching them was going to be a piece of cake, then quit because they didn't want to be seen starting at the bottom.

This makes me sad for many reasons, but the main one is, why worry about what someone else is going to think? Why let someone's opinion still your dream?

We need to put that thinking into check right now, so I want you to memorize this sentence ASAP:

"What you think of me is none of my business."

I repeat,

"*What you think of me is none of my business.*"

Now, this isn't to be memorized with a cocky attitude. This isn't to be memorized by Mr. Ego himself. This is to be memorized so that you can repeat it to yourself every time you feel the opinions of others starting to seep in and make you doubt yourself, because that *will* happen.

There are ways to build a business without having to be ego-driven and step on others to grow.

You don't want to be one of those types of business owners anyway. I know you don't. You want to earn respect and serve with honor, have strong character, and bring value to others. It's that servant's heart that you want to share with the world, and where there is a servant's heart, there is no ego.

Where there is no ego, there is the ability to ask and receive help from others.

Secret revealed…there is more strength in asking for help than in wasting time trying to figure everything out on your own.

It takes a strong person to ask for help and somehow, we've gotten all mixed up. We think asking for help is a sign of weakness. Let me tell you, all the successful business owners I know absolutely recognize that they could not have reached their level of success alone and without help.

So, it's time to get real and raw with yourself and determine how comfortable you are in reaching out for help and admitting you don't have all of the answers all of the time. Think about how you'll react when given constructive criticism and advice from someone you admire and respect. There is a level of maturity required to receive criticism openly and turn it into growth.

A lot of the questions, or thinking points, I have for you in this step are primarily to help you get comfortable with who you are, clear on what you believe, and confident in what you're capable of.

By looking backward and taking inventory of all you have already accomplished, you are able to imagine all you can complete moving forward.

When I looked back at where I was and what things were like when I closed my first business, I was amazed at the strength I had, not only to make the hardest decision of my life, but also to push through and fight for my dream as hard and for as long as I did. I recognized all the tenacity and perseverance that was required of me through that whole process and, you know what, I became proud of myself instead of feeling like I had failed.

I realized that if I got through that and came out just as strong, if not stronger, I definitely had it in me to take on a new business.

I know it's much easier to look back and see all the things you didn't do that you wanted to, but how about we look at all you have done? Think about some of the things you are most proud of.

It makes me think of one of the most common questions in a job interview, one that I'm sure you've been asked before too. It goes like this: "So, tell us, what are you most proud of? What is your greatest accomplishment?"

Do you know how many times, when I was interviewing others, I heard the same answer? "My children. My family." Blah, blah, blah. That would tell me nothing.

Yes, your family is great. They are awesome and you love them tremendously. But I hate to break it to you: the way your children turn out and what they end up doing is going to be on them, and although you may be proud of them, it doesn't tell me anything about your accomplishments.

So, I want you to really think about this for a moment. What are you most proud of? What is your greatest accomplishment? This is about you.

Is it getting out of bed on the mornings when the world would have understood if you crumbled and stayed under your covers?

Is it choosing to get up and still put your red lipstick on when that jerk broke your heart?

Is it getting a job and being able to support your family when the world told you you wouldn't amount to anything because you didn't go to college?

Is it having a whole month where you actually paid your bills on time and didn't lose any sleep over how that was going to happen?

These are not earth-shattering events. These are simple, everyday things that you accomplished that make a difference in your world. Be proud of them.

I will share one of mine with you. I shared it in an interview, too, and I think I surprised the people interviewing me.

When I was asked, "Elena, please tell us what your greatest accomplishment is. What are you most proud of?" this was my actual answer: "Well, I know I should say something like, 'I'm most proud of my kids and being a mom,' but I'm not going to. I am most proud of the moment I received my Women's Entrepreneurial Leadership Award. This award reflected and honored my blood, sweat, and tears. It reflected my work ethic, my effort, my skills, and my heart. That is an accomplishment of mine I am most proud of."

Mic drop! Broken Stronger Bosses aren't afraid to toot their own horns when necessary. Just be sure you're tooting it from your heart and for the right reasons and not because Mr. Ego wants to show off. Get what I'm saying?

Think about not only the things you've accomplished but also the things that life has thrown at you that should have broken you in a moment, but didn't. How did you come out of those times, and how are you better for it today? It is through those moments that I invite you to join me in becoming Broken Stronger.

When life tackles you down with the intention of breaking you to pieces, and yet you pick yourself up and dust yourself off, even if you have to duct tape your frickin' pieces back together – either way, you're able to get back up – you have become Broken Stronger, my friend. Be proud of those moments, just as any other, because those are your accomplishments, too.

Those are the hidden or disguised blessings God put in your life to strengthen you. Only with faith and the ability to hear your inner voice are you able to discern the reason for your pain. Receive that pain as a gift and use it for strength.

All the things that have hurt you in the past are for this very moment. God has been putting you through your own personal training sessions to strengthen you for this very moment because He knows the path of starting a business is not easy. He also knows you can handle it.

Do you think you are frustrated at your job and feel like you're going to explode as you envision your life five years from now doing the exact same thing, by accident? No. God has placed you right where you are and for this very reason.

He has something greater for you being prepared right this very moment and is placing the people, opportunities, ideas, and courage in your path right now to guide you forward.

You are not here by accident. This is your time. You have what it takes.

So, roll up your sleeves, girlfriend, check Mr. Ego at the door, take inventory of all you've survived that didn't break you, and look in the mirror and see your magnificence, your ability, your courage, your beauty, your worth, your potential, your love, your support, and your strength.

As you prepare to embark on this journey, make the decision now to focus on your strength, because you will run into many circumstances that will attempt to break you down. Remind yourself that you've already taken life's best hits and yet, here you are.

You will run into many circumstances where the people who have always loved and supported you will start to treat you differently because you're doing something about your situation and changing as a person. Do it anyway.

You will run into many circumstances that will fight for your attention and try really hard to take you away from your focus and determination. Stay true to your course of action and keep your eye on the prize.

Bottom line, you are going to run into many circumstances that are going to be challenging, but if you're willing to do the work now, you will receive the benefit later.

Take some time to think about how you're going to handle the distractions that try to derail you from your dream. This is an important piece that many don't even consider, but is a guarantee that will happen. It will happen to you.

These outside forces will come at you and if you're prepared for them, they will just tickle you, and you'll laugh in their face. If you're not prepared for them, they will eat you up and make you want to hide.

Things like outgrowing your friends. This will happen. Not with all of them, but with more than you think. Think about it: if you're growing and evolving each day and they are not, how do you expect to stay at the same level? This isn't being cocky or conceited, this is being honest.

How will you handle outgrowing your family? This works in the same way, only this can cut a little deeper. Your family should want to support you and be there for you, no matter what, right? This isn't always the case. They won't understand why you don't want to come out and party. They won't understand why you're not going to spend money on going to a concert. They won't understand why you aren't up to speed on the latest sitcom.

What you are doing will not make sense to many. You will be in a different place and they may start to feel intimidated, whether intentional or not. This won't happen with every person in your family, but I can almost guarantee, it will happen with a few.

How will you handle outgrowing your own life?

There may come a time when what you originally tolerated, you no longer tolerate. You will find yourself in a state of clarity, and focus and this will allow you to see stuff that has been holding you back. It can be shocking. There are going to be a lot of things that shift in your life as you become the person who owns a business instead of being the person who just goes to a job every day.

This shift is okay. It's natural. It's a part of your journey and reflects the strength you have within.

As you grow, so will the challenges you face. It's a forever-ongoing journey. That is why you must love what you do. You have to desire the change you're seeking because you don't ever get to the place where you say "Okay, I've reached my destination. I'm done." It doesn't work that way.

When you accomplish one goal, there will be a new goal on the horizon waiting for you.

Your strength is going to carry you far. Your strength will be replenished by your faith. Faith is the fuel that fills the tanks of strength.

Do not be afraid when weakness sets in. It happens to everyone. You can't keep going and going and going without taking the time to rest and reenergize. The important thing is to recognize when you need this down time and take it. It doesn't mean you are not meant for this journey, it means you are moving at a rapid pace and your tanks are empty. That is all.

Be thankful for those moments because that is proof that progress is being made.

Do not compare your rate of growth with anyone else. You might feel like others who are starting their business are five steps ahead of you. Let them be. They will need their moment to rest and refuel too, and that may be when you're at your peak moment of momentum and progress.

You must want this for you, and for no other reason, because that is what is going to carry you through the moments when you feel like you're having to climb uphill on only fumes.

There is such a joy in the journey if it's what you love, but if you don't love it, it will be chaos and frustration.

I will never lie to you. I will be as honest as I possibly can, even when it hurts, and I'll tell you now, starting a business is not easy. It's not complicated, but it's not easy, because starting a business is more about growing as a person.

As boring as that sounds, it's truth. So many people start out on the path of starting a business and think there are certain things that, if they complete them, they are in business. Those people don't last long. It doesn't matter if you have a logo. It doesn't matter if you have a website. It doesn't matter if you have letterhead. Those are the outside things people see and think that if someone has those, they have a business.

Hate to break it to you, but that is not business. Your business is you. People will want to do business with you because of who you are and how you make them feel. If you are not growing yourself as a person, and learning from others daily, your business will not grow.

You will not reach success simply by having a cool logo.

You are your business. You are what will sell. You are what will draw people in to want to work with you.

Now, can you see how imperative it is that you know yourself, you know why you want this, you know what it is you desire, and that you're able to trust your own inner voice? It's because you are the heart of your business. You are the center that will nurture it and make it blossom into something beautiful. Or, you will keep it confined within the borders of ego and it will suffocate, never having a chance to grow.

CHAPTER 7

Hit That Brick Wall for the Last Time

THE MARIPOSA EFFECT
I – Identify Your Fears

Broken Stronger Boss style, I'm just gonna come out with it…What the heck are you afraid of?

What is it? It's something. It's probably a lot of somethings. What are they?

If not tackled head on, fear can paralyze you and prevent you from moving forward. Fear can stop you in your tracks and make you forget where you're going. Fear can tell you you're crazy for wanting to take another step. Fear will make you second guess yourself and make you feel like you look stupid. Fear will make you afraid of your own success.

I know this because no one is exempt from fear, not even myself.

Fear can be good too, so don't be afraid of it and think of it as only bad.

Establishing a relationship with fear early on will determine the control it has over your life. Once you have a good relationship with fear, you can break free from its holding power and use it only when it's convenient for you. It will no longer control you or your decisions.

I want to you to think about your dream and what it will look like when you're finally done wasting your time at a job you don't love. Can you see it?

Now, what's the worst thing that can happen that will prevent you from getting there?

Aside from you dying, there's not anything. I don't mean to be morbid here, but let's be honest, what is the one and only thing that will stop you from breathing life into your dream? Not having breath – that's the only thing that comes to mind.

It's not ability. You have that.

It's not skill. You have that too, and if there are skills you're lacking, you can learn new ones.

It's not talent. You already have that.

It's not desire or determination. You already have those.

It's not strength. You have that too.

It's not wisdom. You have that and it's growing stronger every day.

So, what are you afraid of that can prevent you from living your dream?

You are afraid that you still don't have what it takes to make your dream come true. If you are reading this book right now, which of course you are, you already have what it takes. You have nothing to fear.

Let's get one thing clear before we move on. Fear and failure are two completely different things.

Most often, there is a fear of failing, so you stay stuck in fear and don't try anything new, so you don't fail. OMG, what a vicious cycle. Failure is nothing to be afraid of. If you're afraid of failing, that's coming from, you guessed it, programming.

You failed a math test, so you are in trouble and now you're grounded. You failed an English test, so you are not smart and will never get into a college. You failed at making the team, so you do not have what it takes to become a part of anything and will be an outcast forever. You failed in a relationship, so there absolutely must be something wrong with you and you're not worthy of love. You failed at saving money, so you must not be responsible and will never have anything nice.

Stop! Stop thinking these things. So, you failed…so what?

People are so afraid to fail that they get stuck in fear and don't want to make decisions. They know they must decide, but because they can't see what's on the other side of Door A or Door B, they don't want to. Let me explain.

You know you must choose either Door A or Door B.

You stare at both doors for a long time. The doors look the exact same, so it's not like one door is prettier than the other. It's not like you're drawn to one door more than you are to the other. So, really it should be an easy decision. Just pick one. But you don't.

You stand there, paralyzed by fear of which door to pick. Thinking if you look long enough, one of the doors will magically open and say, "I am the right choice." That's not gonna happen, so do you know why you are stuck?

You are stuck because of fear of the unknown and the programming you carry inside that tells you that, if you pick the wrong one, you're a failure.

There is no right or wrong one. You're not going to get an F if you choose Door A instead of Door B. It's not a test. It's a choice in life. That is all life is, choices. Life is constant movement forward, and it's moving with or without you. Life is full of opportunity. Opportunity that requires quick decisions.

Because of our programming, we're afraid to make quick decisions because we're afraid they are going to be the wrong ones.

Then we think that if we pick a door and don't like what's behind it, life is unfair. Newsflash: life is neither fair nor unfair, we place that label on it. Life, like I said, is simply constant movement forward, and it's full of opportunity.

It is our own belief system that tells us, through the opinions of others, that this is fair or that is unfair. Life doesn't determine that. People do.

So, back to Door A or Door B. What's it gonna be? It's not difficult. Simply make the choice, open the door, see what's on the other side, and then deal with it.

You get paralyzed and don't want to choose because you're afraid of the work that is on the other side of the door. Brutal honesty at its finest. If you choose Door A, then maybe, just maybe, the work behind it will be easier than the work behind Door B.

Now, you might be thinking, that's not me, I've never taken the easy road. Good for you, but that is still why you're afraid to make the decision. You want to pick the door that will be easier to deal with. The door you know you can easily solve the problem behind, which maybe won't require as much work.

In other words, you want to pick the door that has a problem you already know how to solve because it will make you feel smart and require less effort.

But, if you choose Door B, man, what if there is a bunch of crap behind there that you don't know what to do with? Yes, you will have to learn new things, and it will take you longer to complete, but it doesn't mean it was the wrong door.

Fear comes from not knowing if you have what it takes to successfully complete the to-do's that are sure to come with deciding. You want that security and knowing that you will successfully accomplish all the tasks required – and unfortunately, that is not possible.

You don't have that guarantee when it comes to making a choice, but it still needs to be made. That's why fear creeps in. In all honesty though, what is there to fear? One door will give you the opportunity to learn and grow from new information. Another door will give you a quick success. Either way, you win. And there will always be more doors to open. As soon as you open one, you will see two more, and so on and so on. So be honest about your fear because the doors aren't going to go away.

Common fears are being wrong, failing, looking silly, losing money, being told "I told you so," and doubting yourself. All of these common fears reflect Mr. Ego. Whoa…hello, there's that evil monster again. Ego likes to pop up as often as allowed.

When you can embrace your fear and realize it's not there to work against you, it's there to teach you, then it becomes welcomed. Each time you break through a new level of fear, you gain a new level of confidence and determination and courage. So welcome fear, and then show it who's boss.

Failure is nothing to be afraid of, either. One of the simplest ways to embrace this is to recognize God's unconditional love for you. Realize He loves you so much that there is absolutely nothing you can do in this world that will break His love for you.

You don't earn more love by doing good or choosing the right door. You don't lose love by making a wrong decision and choosing the wrong door.

God placed both doors in your path and gives you the freedom to choose. If He placed them both there, how can one be wrong, and how can you be punished for choosing the wrong one when there is no wrong one?

I want you to absorb that for a moment. When you're faced with all sorts of decisions when it comes to leaving your job, starting your business, and becoming your own boss, there are no failures ahead of you so great that they will prevent you from achieving your dream.

There will be lessons along the way, sure, but let's face it, if you had all the knowledge, information, and know-how when it comes to starting your business already, you wouldn't be wasting your time at a job you hate.

So, kick fear in the booty and make the decisions you know you need to.

There is always something to be learned from the failures in our life. You might be thinking, yeah, I was a dumb donkey for making that stupid choice, but I bet you learned from it and won't make it again.

You might be thinking, yeah, that was another time I made a stupid decision…but remember, you survived, and people still love you right?

So, what is so bad about making a decision that may not turn out to be the best one? Nothing. You learn, and you grow from every failure in your life.

As you get more comfortable with failure, you realize it always brings with it a gift. You learn more. You gain more confidence. You move on to the next decision much faster. You fail mindfully and with purpose. You fail looking for the lesson, get back up, and try again.

Maybe long ago you used failure as an excuse to stop working toward your dream. Maybe you once told yourself, "Yeah, I tried that. It didn't work." But that's not you anymore.

Successful people don't dodge failure and they aren't exempt from failure. Instead, they look for the failure much sooner, so they can quickly discover what will bring success.

So, if you're feeling like you know leaving your job is the right step for you and starting a business is the right step for you, but you're afraid to fail…girlfriend, you can only fail if you quit working toward your dream. You can only fail if you don't even begin.

There is no failure in trying. There is no failure in making mistakes. There is no failure in getting back up and trying again. Remember, if you try something and it fails, what you tried failed…but you are not a failure. There is a big difference.

The fears that you hold within yourself are going to define the level of success you can achieve.

Fear only has power if you give it power, and fear and failure go hand in hand.

Failure is a part of learning and anyone who is climbing their personal ladder of success is in a constant state of learning. So, get comfortable with failing. It's how you grow.

If you are not learning daily and find yourself surrounded by people who think they have all the answers, you're in the wrong place.

We all know that not every decision is going to be the right one, but there is a comfort in working with someone who you know is not afraid to make a bad decision because they will learn from it, grow, and move on to the next decision. The key is that they are still climbing and pushing forward.

When it comes to working with mentors, I can tell you that there is not a whole lot of energy that will be put into you if you are afraid and remain paralyzed in fear. Ouch.

So, I need you to get raw and ask yourself where you stand on your comfort level with fear. How afraid are you of failing?

Be honest with yourself. This is the most common obstacle and one of the hardest to work through because it's been programmed in people for as long as they can remember. People are programmed to believe it is bad to fail. It is not!

You will have to rewire your thinking and train your brain to feel differently about fear and failure. You will need to embrace failure and make it your friend.

In business, failure will be with you on a regular basis so it's best to strengthen your relationship with fear and failure now. Take inventory of the things you've tried that hurt you or that you feel you failed at.

It could be someone from your past who told you that you would never amount to anything. It could be someone from your past that told you that you could be anything you wanted, but when it came down to it, didn't support you.

It's time to look in the mirror and take ownership of who you are, what you want, and what God has planned for you and your life. Do not be afraid. Do not fear failing.

Those that love you and are closest to you may not understand why you want to do what you want to do. That's ok, they don't have to, but if they love you, they will want to support you and honor who you are as a person.

One of my favorite quotes that I am reminded of right now is, "You don't need to understand me to love me, but you do need to love me to understand me." I read it years ago, and it has been imprinted in my mind ever since.

The same goes for you. Those that love you should understand you and the journey you need to take for yourself. They may not understand the journey, but they should be willing to understand.

So, look fear in the face and plow forward. It doesn't stand a chance against God's unconditional love for you.

Oh, and one more thing: there is absolutely nothing you can fail at that will prevent you from becoming all that you were created to be.

CHAPTER 8

Unleash Your Power

THE MARIPOSA EFFECT
P – Propel Your Thoughts

Buckle up Buttercup because this is one chapter you're either going to get right away, or you're going to read and say, "Whaaaat?"

All your success resides within the six inches between your ears – give or take an inch, depending on how big your head is. Seriously though, the most important factor of success begins in your mind.

It's not having the prettiest website, the most creative logo, the fanciest letterhead, the most unique business card, or even a powerful business name. None of those things will bring success. Success first begins in your mind.

We couldn't start talking about your mind until you knew the importance of having a desire, and until we reached your heart, and you began to trust your voice inside.

You've also been able to see how strong you are and all that you've already accomplished. Plus, you now know that there is absolutely nothing to be afraid of.

So, now it's time to bring it all together and explain how the mind will make all the difference.

I'm going to be honest with you: this information you're receiving is extremely powerful. It will change the design of your future, but only if you work on it.

It's not a deep hidden secret that your mind and your thoughts can give you the outcome you desire. It's because most people don't slow down enough to process this information and put it into practice that makes it seem so foreign.

Question every successful person out there, and they will be able to tell you about the power their thoughts played in their success.

So, if you are ready to take power over your life and begin to design the future you desire, receive this information and act on it. This is information a positional leader will not accept. That is why that type of leader will never excel on their own; they will remain behind their title while working for someone else.

There could be a whole book written on just this chapter topic alone, and I'm sure there are many out there. I'm not going to go into every detail, because right now you just want to know that you have what it takes to start your own business, right?

Let me ask you this: do you believe you can start your own business? Note: I didn't ask you how, and I didn't ask you when. I asked, "Do you believe you can?"

As cliché as it sounds, you become what you believe. So, if you don't believe you can, you won't. If you believe you can, you will. How, you wonder? There is a cycle to how every thought becomes your reality. Scary, huh?

Let's break it down, and again, this is in its simplest form because I don't like to overcomplicate things.

Divide your brain in half. You have a conscious side and a subconscious side.

Okay, good. Easy enough.

Conscious is what we'll call the thinking side. It's either black or white; you either did or you didn't, it's up or it's down, you either can or you can't, you will or you won't. It's the side that thinks logically.

For example, if something is left outside in the rain, it will get wet. If you don't want it to get wet, you make the choice to bring it inside. If you don't fill the tank with gas, your car will not go anywhere. So, if you have someplace to be and you are low on gas, you choose to stop at the gas station and fill up your tank. If there is no air in the bicycle tire, and you want to go for a bike ride, you choose to put more air in your tire so you can go. The conscious mind is where you do your thinking and where your decisions should be made.

Now, subconscious mind is entirely different. The subconscious is where feelings and emotions are held. It's the subconscious mind that makes you "feel" a certain way about something. It's also on, and functioning automatically, all the time. It never shuts off. This is the side of your brain that controls your breathing, and thank goodness it never shuts off because can you imagine if we had to control and think about our breathing? We'd all be dead in about five seconds flat! Especially those that think they're excellent multi-taskers. Multi-taskers would be an extinct breed in no time.

Subconscious is on all the time, even while you sleep. It holds feelings and emotions. It receives everything as truth.

Now, you might find that you make decisions from your subconscious side, from how you feel, and this is such a no no. Think about how often your feelings and emotions change in just a day. Even in an hour, you can feel completely differently about something than you did earlier. At least, I know I can. Therefore, it is important to train yourself to make decisions from the conscious part of your brain, instead of the subconscious part.

Are we good? Alright, let's keep going.

It is your feelings and emotions that drive your actions. Get your highlighter out and highlight that last sentence right now. It's so good, I have to repeat it…it is your feelings and emotions that drive your actions.

How you feel about something controls what you do about it. So, if you don't like something, or it makes you feel uncomfortable, notice how it sits there and you dread getting to it. You don't feel like doing it. You don't want to do it, so you don't, or you put it off.

But if it makes you feel good, you can't wait to get started.

So, let's continue to take this full circle.

It is then your actions that drive your results. Your actions are what give you the results you're seeking.

Let's break this down.

Say, you don't know if you should start a business. You are in limbo because right now you're thinking about it, not from your conscious mind, but from your subconscious. You're paying attention to how you feel about it already. It's your feelings that are telling you if you can or you can't, right?

The way you are feeling about starting your business is false information because you have nothing to base it off of. You haven't even begun, so there is no data to compare or gauge from, but you're already shooting yourself down or giving yourself the reasons why you probably shouldn't, based on how you feel or how others feel.

If you consciously look at the decision from fact-based information, you'll quickly realize that it is quite possible. It's simply a choice, a decision that yes, you are going to start a business. You then begin with taking one step, and then another, and then another. Your conscious mind knows that starting your business is just a series of decisions that need to be made and acted upon. That's it.

So, how do we transfer this doubt into confidence? Know that with faith anything is possible and if you are in the state of desire, there is no stopping you. Just decide, are you going to start a business or are you not going to start a business?

This isn't one of those things where you get to say, "Well, I'll do a few starter things, and if it seems like it's going to move in the right direction, then I will go all in and keep working on it." That right there is the formula for "don't even start."

If you can't decide with a clean yes or no that are you are going to become a business owner, then don't do it. I'm being brutally honest because I want you to be successful. If your mind is already doubting that it will work for you, then it probably won't. Or it will take a lot longer because you most certainly have a lot more growth to do around your mindset. Do yourself a favor and forget about starting a business until you get right in the mind and believe that you can; otherwise, you're just wasting more of your precious time.

If you're ready, then start referring to yourself as a business owner in your own mind. Your subconscious receives everything as truth. Everything. It doesn't think and pick and choose, it feels on whatever you give it and receives it all as truth. Therefore, major decisions shouldn't be made off of feeling.

Diverting for a minute here to give you an example…

How many people are in relationships they know they should not be in but stay because they feel they can't leave? I'll just leave that right there. My point is, we have all made wrong decisions that we knew were not the right ones for us, but we made them anyway because of how we were feeling. Don't do that in business.

When you start thinking of yourself as a business owner, you'll start thinking like a business owner. You'll begin to do the research and work required, search for the knowledge you're missing, and begin to ask people who are already successful how to do what they did. All the things you want and need to know in order to learn how to start and run your business will become a priority to you. You will have a drive, an urgency, a desire to get started and succeed. It's this feeling and emotion that will push you into action and it's those actions that will give you the results you're seeking, to be your own boss.

So, it's a full cycle.

Think > Feel > Do > Be

There is a study that tells us that our subconscious isn't fully developed until we are about five to seven years old. That is why you learned how to walk even though you fell a million times and possibly hurt yourself. You weren't afraid. You didn't overthink and overanalyze why you fell, why you bumped your head on the coffee table, why you skinned your knee on the carpet. No, you got up and tried walking again until your mother couldn't keep up with you anymore.

Think about it. You didn't feel any way about it. You didn't make your decision about whether you were going to continue to learn how to walk based on how you felt about the number of times you fell. You just did it. This was your subconscious leading you. It receives everything as truth, and you saw other people walking around and knew you could, too. You didn't doubt yourself, you weren't capable of overthinking. Your conscious mind wasn't developed yet.

Our subconscious doesn't question, it just accepts. So, if you tell yourself you are successful, subconscious says, okay, I'm successful and you begin feeling this way; therefore, your actions will reflect how you feel, and those actions will give you results.

It's a full circle.

So, tell yourself right now, "I can do this. I have what it takes to start my own business. I will be my own boss. I will be successful. I will have all that my heart desires, and I will listen to the ideas that are in my head. I am already equipped with everything I need to succeed. God made me perfectly and abundantly, and I will prosper. I will become a successful business owner. I will leave my job when the moment is aligned. I will have an exit plan to leave my job.

My business will be in existence by the time I leave my job. I will have the support I need to start my business."

Keep on going, start saying all the things you believe. There is power in your words.

I will share one thing with you: I believe in you. I have full confidence that you can, and will, start the business of your dreams, and when you do, you will succeed and prosper. The fact that you are reading this book now tells me that you are already ready. You just needed to catch up to yourself. You have already decided you are ready, or you would have never purchased this book.

OMG, I am so excited for you.

So, a few things to work on immediately. Change your thinking. People overcomplicate this one all the time. It's not always easy, but it is simple.

Change your thinking, change your life.

If you tell yourself you're tired, guess what? You're going to be more tired.

If you tell yourself you don't have money, guess what? You will never have money.

If you tell yourself you don't have time, guess what? You will never have time.

You speak truth into your life. When you turn your self-talk around, you turn your world around.

Here are some powerful starters…

Instead of telling yourself you don't have money, tell yourself ,"With the money I have, I choose not to spend it on [blank] right now." That is taking control over your situation. When you tell your money what you are doing with it, it will obey. It's a moving energy, so if you don't control it, it will move, and you will have no idea where it went.

This might sound crazy, but I talk to my money. I tell it that I appreciate it. That I love how it helps take care of me and my family. That I don't want to ever take it for granted, so if I ever make it feel that way, I am sorry. That I will protect it, and it is safe with me. I tell my money that I want it to grow so that I can help serve more people. My money knows we have a partnership, and I will do my part so it can do its part.

It's taken me a lot of years, and even some therapy, to understand money and my relationship with it. This is how much the mind can impact your life. I told you how I grew up with parents that were entrepreneurs, and very successful ones at that, and there was a lot of money. I grew up not needing much of anything, but I was never spoiled. There's a difference.

I went to kindergarten in a mink coat, and I was embarrassed by that because I wanted a puffy plastic coat like all my friends had. I still have the coat, by the way. It's at my mom's and it serves more as a symbol for me, a reminder to stay humble and that money doesn't buy happiness.

I also had a large ruby ring in the first grade, and I was terrified when I had to tell my dad I lost it on the playground because it slid off my finger when I was hanging on the monkey bars. I searched and searched after school in the tiny gravel hoping I would find it, but I didn't. I'll never forget the sound of his dropping fork clanking on the plate at dinner when I told him I lost it. My point here is that I had a lot of things most young kids don't have, but then one day...it was gone. Not just the money was gone, but so was my dad...so was my family.

It took me years to understand that it wasn't the money or the success that broke my family apart. It was alcoholism. My dad liked beer, a lot of it. The more money and success came his way, the more he partied, etc. That is what broke my family apart, but I didn't know that until many years later. I always thought it was having money and businesses and being so busy that broke my family apart, so I was afraid of my own success. I was afraid to make too much money. I was afraid to get too busy. All the things I thought broke my family apart, I didn't want to welcome into my own family.

This is how your mind has the power to design your life. My own fears and beliefs were pushing away the things that would allow me to financially take care of my family, but I was afraid to receive them. I was causing my own problems and frustrations, blocking the blessings that were mine to have out of fear of something that didn't even exist.

I had to work for years, and it's still a conscious practice every day, to openly receive financial success and know it is not going to break my family apart.

So, my friend, begin to take control of your financial situation by simply choosing to think differently about the money you do have, and speak differently about it, and watch how things begin to turn around for you.

The same goes for time. Instead of telling yourself that you don't have time, tell yourself, "Right now it's not a priority of mine, but when it becomes a priority, I will do it."

Any time you tell yourself you don't have time, you're really stating it's not important to you. Trust me, if it were important, you would do it.

It boils down to this: it's time to stop lying to yourself and talking like a victim. Ouch.

I am going to be brutally honest, once again, because that is the only way you will get to success. You don't need someone who will just tell you what you want to hear surrounding you right now. You also don't need someone who can help you in this process, hold your hand every time you say you can't. No, you need someone who is going to keep pushing you, saying yes you can, so get to climbing.

See yourself owning your business. See yourself making decisions. See yourself smiling. See yourself surrounded by people listening to you and your ideas.

We think in pictures, so see yourself successful. This will draft your thoughts. Your thoughts will become feelings and your feeling will drive your actions. Before you know it, you will have the results you want, simply by seeing it right now.

When my little voice started telling me I had to leave my job, I knew right then that I had to decide. I had to decide that I had grown all I was gonna grow at my job and there was no one else there I could really learn from, so I had to leave. I didn't leave for several months after deciding, but by making my choice, it drove all my actions and, months later, I had the results. I left my job.

It was a lot of work during the few months of my transition, but it was a structured and organized transition because of the series of decisions I made.

There is nothing different about me and you. There is no reason you can't do what I did. I am not more special than you, I am not smarter or more gifted. We are all equals, we are just in different phases of our journey.

Keep in mind that if you speak negativity over your life, you will have negativity in your life. But if you speak positivity over your life, you will have positivity in your life. It really is that simple.

It's programming that needs to be reprogrammed. You pretty much have to undo all you know to relearn and to grow.

Knowing how your mind works is going to change the way you see things. It might even be sad to see people you love think and create negative circumstances into their own lives. You can't undo this thinking now. You are fully aware that you can change the design of your future by your very own thoughts.

So, when the time comes that you're feeling stuck, and it will, remind yourself that you have to think your way into results.

Think > Feel > Do > Be.

CHAPTER 9

Sometimes It's Better to Be the Listener

THE MARIPOSA EFFECT
O – Optimize Your Connections

We've covered some very complex steps in the process of determining whether starting a business is right for you. I know you may be thinking, these are non-traditional things, or things you may not have considered when thinking about what it takes to start a business. That's good. We do things non-traditionally so we can have non-traditional results.

These are all critical, non-negotiable steps that make for a solid and firm foundation for success. These are the fundamentals that will carry you throughout every decision you're going to need to make in business, and will determine whether people want to work with you and for you, which ultimately is what drives success.

Like you heard me say earlier, it's not about the website, it's not about the logo, or any of those outward items. That does not make or break a successful business. What is going to determine success is you, your relationship with yourself, how you think in your own mind, and how you conquer the personal obstacles along the way.

You can hire people to help with every outward aspect of business, but you, Broken Stronger Boss, are something that cannot be duplicated. Therefore, invest in yourself, your growth, and your mindset. That is where you will receive the greatest return on investment when it comes to scaling your business to the top. It is about you!

Now, while you're sitting at your job, hating every moment, I'm sure you haven't given much thought to how to make people gravitate toward wanting to work with you, help you, listen to you, and respect you – but you will want to.

The key is connect, don't communicate. I know this may sound ridiculous, but so many people think they are great communicators just because they like to talk. Don't be one of those types, be a good connector.

Connecting with others is what will give your business stability and steady growth.

People know people, and if you are connected, people will recommend you. If you're constantly talking at people, they will run and never come back. So, let's get clear on the difference between communicating and connecting.

Communicating is an exchange of words. And, most likely, not a clear exchange. Only a small portion of the words heard are ever retained and acted on. Communicating usually means one person is doing the talking and asks if anyone has questions, and usually no one does, because no one is really listening or invested in the topic.

Connecting is an exchange of spirit and energy. It's a tie that will bind you to another person on a deeper level. Connecting comes from asking questions and listening.

When you're connected with others, everyone is engaged. Everyone is included and feels important and like a priority. When connected, everyone contributes more to the task at hand and the results become far greater than you could have imagined.

Therefore, it's so important to begin connections when starting a business, rather than just going around and talking to people. Not everyone wants to hear about your dream and vision. Another ouch!

Once you have connected with someone, they will want to hear you dream and vision and want to know what they can do to help. If you go around just telling people what you want, they will say "good for you and good luck" and be on their merry way.

One of the fastest ways to connect with someone is to build rapport. The quickest way to build rapport with someone is to mimic their behavior.

For example, if they are sitting across from you with one arm on the table and sort of lean to one side in their chair, do the same. Don't be weird about it, though. Just slightly move your way into the same position to mirror them. This will position the person across from you to feel more comfortable. They will feel at ease and not even know why.

Another way to build rapport with someone is to use some of the same language they use. This might seem crazy too, but if they like to cuss, then feel free to say some cuss words. If they like to use bigger words, pull your bigger words out of your back pocket, too. Of course, make sure you know how to use them appropriately!

If they take their jacket off, take yours off too. If they cross their leg, cross yours. It's about recognizing the little nuances they have and discreetly mirroring them. It may take a few minutes into the conversation to begin to build this rapport because you don't want to do everything they do right when they do it, or they'll look at you and wonder when the game of Simon Says began and things will feel odd. So, when I say discreetly, it means take your time, be subtle, and make your movements flow. You want the movement that you're mimicking to look like it's your own. If it's not something you're comfortable with, don't do it. I am not a fan of crossing my legs because it hurts my knees, so that is not something I will use as a mirror move because I look very uncomfortable when I try to cross my legs. But if my potential client has her elbows on the table, I will put mine on the table as well. If she has hers off the table, I will keep mine off the table, too. It's little things.

This approach can be used in any setting and with anyone that you want to feel connected to and build rapport quickly.

When you use this approach, especially during a meeting, the person you meet with will leave feeling like they've known you forever. They will describe you to someone else like this, "I don't know what it was about her, but I feel like I can trust her. I feel like I've known her all my life or like I can just be myself around her."

Those may not be the exact words, but you get the idea.

When you build rapport with someone, and quickly, they will be drawn to you and they won't know why. But here's why: it's because you remind them of themselves, and everyone loves themselves.

One of the other ways to connect with someone is to recognize what type of personality they are right away. There is so much involved in this topic that it could be a book all in itself; however, I feel so strongly about the importance of understanding others' personalities for the success of your business, and in life, that I want to share some key points.

There are a few indicators that can signal what type of person you are dealing with right away.

Introductions

If someone introduces themself and uses their first and last name, they are going to be more formal and you should be as professional as possible throughout the whole interaction.

If someone introduces themself and uses their first name only, they do better with a more casual approach. They feel like your friend already. So, if they say, "Hi, I'm Amy. Nice to meet you," Amy is probably more of a down-to-earth person, a bit more relaxed, and just wants to have real talk.

Apparel

If they have a lot of black or dark solid colors, maybe even some bling, they are going to be more power-driven and again, a bit more formal. It may take a little bit longer to build rapport and connection, but once you do, you're good.

If they have a lot of trendy-looking styles, with bold prints and patterns and even a little bit of an edgy hairstyle, etc. they are more laid back. They are the ones who want to be more of your friend and will connect with you much more quickly.

Voice

There are people who, no matter how excited they are about a subject, simply speak in such a monotone voice that it will put you to sleep. These types of people are more fact- and research-driven; they don't have much fluctuation or animation in their voices during a conversation. It's more of a rhythmic, unemotional delivery. Those types of people don't want to hear your story. They don't care if your product worked for someone else. They want to know the facts and can drill you with questions all day long.

If someone is very animated with their voice, and may even talk with their hands, they want to know the whole story and have no problem telling you theirs. These people are easily convinced to try something new. They most likely have been up late at night and bought a vacuum and pots and pans off an infomercial simply because it changed someone's life for the better.

A lot of times, the more friendly, outgoing, trendy folks who want to be your friend are the creative people who love to start projects but rarely finish them, unless they find the project to be a lot of fun.

The more serious and dark suited people are the ones who will see to it that the project is complete and will attempt to do it better than anyone else could have. Warning: they may not look like they're having a lot of fun along the way.

So, keeping your task at hand and the reason for building the connection clear will help you determine which type of people you want to meet with right away. Knowing this in advance will save you a lot of time and bring you positive results much sooner.

It may not always be the same type of person that you need to work with. It will really be based on the project and the result you are seeking.

It's also good to know what motivates your people, clients, and customers.

If someone is motivated by fun, a monetary reward is not going to encourage them to work harder. If someone is motivated by money, a plaque with their name on it is going to end up in the trash and not push them to work harder. Different things motivate different types of people, so if you're giving your people the wrong things to encourage them, it will backfire.

This includes yourself. Are you clear on what motivates you?

Do you like to treat yourself to something fun if you accomplish a goal? Do you like to finish first and at the top of your game and know you made the most money? Or do you like to feel a sense of satisfaction that comes with knowing you have helped someone by the work you do? Be honest with yourself. None of these are right or wrong. It's who you are, and it's important to know what motivates you, especially when leading yourself.

I will be very honest here, if you have not received your college degree, you are most likely motivated by fun or by being at the top of your game. So much so, that you felt your way was better. And it was suffocating to you to sit in a classroom with tons of people who were content to blend in and not think for themselves.

I am one of those, so it's nothing to be ashamed of. Being one who is motivated by being the best I can be and to reward myself with something fun is what has allowed me to break away from my mundane life of working the same job for someone else, every single day. It has served me well, so if that is where you find yourself…own it.

Connecting will make such a huge difference in the way others perceive your business, too. It's the difference between people saying they really like and respect what it is you're doing or deciding to stay away because they are made to feel intimidated.

So, be very honest about how well you connect with others. This is an area that is worth working on if it's not one of your strong points.

This is also another place Mr. Ego likes to show up and can really mess things up.

Because you are ready and able to start a business does not make you better than anyone else. It makes you a person who listened to her inner voice, acknowledged her strength, crushed her fears, and took control of her mind and her decisions…but not better than anyone else.

People will want to be a part of what you're doing when you are openly able to admit that you need help. No one starts out in business with the know-how in every aspect, and it's the ones who are afraid to ask for help, or afraid to be seen starting at the bottom, who don't get very far.

Connect with people. You need people. Open yourself up, ask questions. At this stage, it is better to listen than it is to talk. Collect information and gain knowledge; this will give you more credibility rather than coming out of the gate acting like you know how to do it all already. If you did, you wouldn't need this book.

I say these things to you because I believe in pushing you to be the very best you can be, and that very best is usually hidden behind fear and/or ego. I had people push me, and I wouldn't be where I am today if I acted like I knew it all. Believe me.

One more thing about connecting, and probably the most important piece, is it must be genuine. You must really want to connect with people. You can't fake it.

People who are already in tune with themselves and on a high level of independence and success have a very keen sense of self and a strong level of discernment and wisdom. They will spot insincerity from a mile away. They will spot someone trying to be something they are not. They will spot negative intention. Don't be that person. It must be genuine.

Make sure your motives are right, your intentions are pure, and you're truly coming from a humble place of service. In a book I read years ago, *The Ideal Team Player*, there are three components that make an ideal team player:

Humble. Hungry. Smart. Meaning, if you can encompass all three of these characteristics, people will want to work with you. This will make you ideal to others.

Stay humble. No one is better than the other. Everyone knows something you don't. If you're in a room where you feel like you know the most, get yourself into a different room where you can start learning again.

This is what happens in a lot of corporations. Leaders get to a high level and forget they should still be learning. They aren't looking for new ways to solve old problems. So, instead, they keep doing what they've always done, and therefore, people leave because there is no opportunity for personal growth and new learning. Don't be this type of boss.

Lock arms with the people around you. Do your part to hold each other up and raise each other to higher levels. It is much more fulfilling and rewarding to grow your business knowing you have a team behind you that you treat equally and with respect.

You might start out solo, but you will see very quickly that even starting out on your own will require others. You will want to have an idea of who your ideal team players are.

Stay hungry. Stay in the zone of working for more. More growth, more knowledge, more understanding, more connections, more opportunities, etc.

When you start feeling bored or defeated, or doubt seeps in, all these things will steal your hunger away. It's important to keep yourself in a position of being challenged so you're in constant state of growth and learning. No one should want your business to succeed more than you. So, if you aren't hungry for success, learning, and growing, move away from the table. It won't work.

Take a break if you need, but do not quit. Stay hungry. Find what you need, and then do the work.

Be smart. Train yourself to think logically, not emotionally, and look several steps ahead.

In business, you want to always see a few steps ahead of you and take one step each day. Connect with people and branch out to find people who have what you want, so you can do what they do. Connect with them. Remember to take caution though when selecting who to connect with and who to go to for advice. That is so important to remember. I repeat it often, because people are going to give you their opinion and advice from their own level of awareness, and it is that level of awareness that has brought them to where they are in their life. So be willing to trade positions with anyone you consider asking for advice.

So, when you find the people who have what you want, join their groups or watch their videos. Hire them to work with you. Connect. Don't worry, you are worthy. No one is better than you, you're just at different phases of your journey, remember?

You will have friends you'll want to share your stories with about what you're doing or thinking. Word of advice: hold off on that for a while. They will fill your mind with things it doesn't need, because they are not going to understand your journey.

Here's a true story of mine to show you what I mean. When I decided to leave my corporate leadership position, I gave a four-month notice. Now, keep in mind that I had been putting my plan in place for much longer. But when the news got out, the first thing I was asked was, "Aren't you scared?"

Because of my mindset, I was already prepared for this type of question to come at me, and so I was able to confidently answer, "No. I'm not."

Had I not been prepared, I may have allowed fear to creep into my head and make me second guess my decision. I was able to answer confidently because I knew the success I was worthy of receiving already resided within me. I knew the journey I was choosing to take was the right one for me, and I would succeed. Now, I may not have known exactly what the journey was going to look like or the twists and turns it was going to take, but I wasn't scared, and I knew if I let those thoughts start entering my mind, they would grow, and I'd end up becoming scared and questioning myself.

I share this with you because if you start sharing your thoughts and ideas before you are confident in them, people will get into your head and you will doubt yourself. Even friends and family will make you doubt yourself if you allow them.

Let me make one thing clear: I didn't always have this confidence and mindset I have today. I wasn't always confident in my decisions and abilities, and I certainly screwed up enough times to become very close friends with failure. Sometimes the biggest doubts you carry in your mind come from those who are closest to you and love you the most.

When I took my entry level job at the corporation I worked for after closing my business and applied for the promotion and got it after only twelve weeks, someone very close to me said, "Do you think you got that promotion on your own? I'm sure it's because some of your family works at that corporation." Wow…enter self-doubt.

Yes, I had a family member that worked there too, but there were over twelve thousand employees overall. I'm sure the one that I knew was not the reason I got the promotion, but I let that idea marinate in my head for a long time, and I felt unworthy. I started doubting my ability. I started wondering, "Is that why I got the promotion? Do I not have skills?" I knew the answer, but that's the kind of ugliness that can seep into your mind and thoughts and turn into belief, if you let it.

Surround yourself and connect with people who leave you feeling better about yourself. When you surround yourself with the right kind of leaders, you always walk away feeling taller. Average people want to keep you average. Small people want to bring you down.

Connect with those that lift you up and use your uniqueness as the superpower it is.

CHAPTER 10

Lead the Way

THE MARIPOSA EFFECT
S – Strengthen Your Influence

Do you know how to lead yourself?

Until you can lead yourself with confidence and ease, you can't lead others with confidence and ease.

There is a definite difference between positional leadership and servant leadership. Many people claim to know the difference, but rarely know the differences in detail.

Let's start with the easy one: positional leadership.

A positional leader is simply someone who states they are a leader because they have a title after their name that says they are a leader.

They may not possess one skill of true leader, but because they have the title, they are a leader. This is one that gets under my skin and one I saw too many times in my corporate position.

Over the years, I've seen this happen because there are people who do a very good job in their roles. They have a high skill level when it comes to the tasks of their jobs. They know the work duties and work hard. Then a leadership position becomes available, they apply, and because of their history of doing their job well, they are selected. They may not have one stinkin' clue about what is required to lead another team member, they just did their job well.

So, now that they are a leader and they are the boss, almost immediately Mr. Ego prances in with his smirky grin and the team quickly falls apart.

I'm sorry, I don't care how much you try to convince me, a title does not make a leader.

If you don't know how to connect with people, if you don't know how to control your mind and thought process, if you don't know how to discern the wisdom that is coming from your inner voice, if you don't know how to conquer the fears that are going to stare at you in the face every day, you are not going to be able to successfully lead a team to progress.

You may be able to boss them around, but they will eventually leave because they will not want to work for you.

Servant leadership, on the other hand, is what makes me all warm and gooey inside. It is also often misunderstood.

When people who want to be a boss hear "servant leadership," they roll their eyes and think, "I want to be the boss, not a servant."

Servant leadership is about making required decisions that will not only benefit the goals of the business, but also the goals of the individual. It's about feeding some of your selflessness into others to raise them up. It's about setting the right type of boundaries to keep progress moving forward and steering those that get off track back in line.

Think of a child who hates brushing their teeth before bed. You are serving them well by remaining committed to the task of brushing their teeth every night, even if it's met with moaning and groaning, every frickin' night. You are serving your child (and their teeth) well.

Servant leadership isn't giving everyone everything want they want all the time and never saying no or making uncomfortable decisions. No, it's keeping things in line for the betterment of both the business and the individual.

Servant leadership is the one way that you can be sure to influence your team and peers to want to work with you.

As you begin focusing on leadership, because that is a staple of business, it's important to be honest and realize the one person who is going to be the hardest to lead is yourself.

This is a very big adjustment to get comfortable with when becoming your own boss.

There won't be anyone else to make sure you complete your work by a certain deadline. There won't be anyone else to hold you accountable to do all the things you have to do. There won't be anyone else to make sure you are staying creative and coming up with new and innovative ways to do business. There isn't going to be anyone else who is going to make sure you keep stretching beyond your comfort zone and continuously connecting with new people.

Leading yourself is just like leading anyone else; get clear on when you're most productive.

Take inventory of when you have the most energy. For some it's in the morning and others it's in the evening. For me, it's late at night. Some people like keeping their calendar in their phone or computer, others like to have a paper calendar and write every appointment down. On top of that, some like to write in their calendars with different colored pens.

Some of these things sound silly to think about, but here's the thing. When you are starting out on anything new, you pick up and read just about anything you can get your hands on to learn.

You'll read articles that talk about millionaires who wake up at four thirty a.m. every day to get their hour of workout in and their hour of reading or writing in before anyone wakes up.

So, you think…okay, I need to start waking up super early to get things done like these other millionaires. And after hitting your snooze button for the fifth time, you wake up already feeling like a failure and like you will never have what it takes to become a millionaire yourself.

If you work better late at night, who's to say you can't? If that's what works for you, go for it.

If you like to color code when others suggest making bullet points…color code.

The main thing is, do you know how you work and work productively?

One of my clients came to me and had been working in a direct sales marketing clothing business, and as the rules of the company were changing, they were changing to no longer align with my client's values. She was frustrated because she felt stuck. She was torn because she really liked fashion and wanted to have her own business, but knowing who she was and what she wanted, this company was no longer the right fit. We worked through several things and, fast forward almost a year, she now has her own clothing boutique and is running her business according to her values, her vision, and with her heart.

Had she not taken the time to take inventory of how she worked and what type of leader she wanted to be in her own business and to others, she may have never recognized that the frustration she was feeling each day in the previous company she was a part of was because it wasn't aligned with her values. If she didn't know this, she may have just thought she was a bad business owner.

By knowing this information, we were quickly able to come to a solution and put the steps in place to allow her to continue to live her dream in fashion, but kick it up a notch and open her very own boutique, her very own way. And you know what, she is a very successful business owner and completely in her zone of genius. She's there because she knew herself enough to know when she was not there. There are times you may not know what the right fit is, but you know where you are isn't it.

You must be solid in your image of yourself; otherwise, you'll see bits and pieces of success in others and want to compare yourself. You will beat yourself down for not being as good as them or not doing things the same as them.

So, learn to lead yourself first. Be honest with yourself. If there are things you want to do differently, things you know are not assets to the success you want, identify them and then change them.

Leadership is about how you make others feel. So, teach your team and peers the same. Holding onto information for yourself, thinking it will give you power or a one up over others, will backfire. That's what positional leaders do. They are afraid to share the good stuff because they are afraid someone is going to come in and knock them off their throne.

A true leader knows that the greatness of the team, the success of the business, is only as good as the people who pour their heart and soul into it.

So why would you not want to share awesome information with anyone and everyone you choose to work with? It will raise the level of everyone in your circle, and this, my friend, is how your business will excel at a much greater speed than someone thinking they know it all and can do it all on their own.

A question that is often asked in job interviews is, "In your career, who has been a good leader and why?" The person asking this question is trying to see what type of characteristics stand out to you as good leadership qualities.

I want you to take a moment and think about this question, too. In your current situation, since you feel you are wasting valuable time at your job (the reason why you bought this book), why are you feeling this way?

What have your bosses done to make you feel like your time is being wasted? How have they treated you? How have they communicated with you? Have they connected with you? Where do you feel they fail as a servant leader? These are all things to consider when setting out and starting your own business.

Pay attention to why you feel the way you do, and what can be done to ensure you never make someone feel the same way.

Society moves so fast, there is often little time spent analyzing ourselves. Everyone seems to be walking around out there looking for ways to blame others and point fingers for why they are feeling the way they are.

You are different. You are going to take that time to look at yourself and analyze why you are wasting valuable time at your job and what it is that is telling you that you are ready to break free.

I would encourage you to make a list of things you like about your current boss or previous bosses who have made an impact on you, and things you do not like.

Determine the characteristics you like that you feel you possess, and be honest with yourself about the ones you don't have.

I remember when I was starting out, I thought there was something negative about being categorized in the group that wanted to be the best, was motivated by money, that wanted only the best and finest of everything. I remember thinking, "How can I be categorized in this group, when I don't see myself in any of that?"

What I was really saying was that I had been exposed to those types of people who used their power in a negative way, and I didn't want to be associated with them. The type of people I had met like that were quick to step on anyone they needed to get to where they were going. I thought, *please do not put me in this category.*

Here's the thing, though: after learning about choices and how the mind works, I welcomed these attributes, but I made the choice about the type of person I was going to be.

Do I want to be the best? Yes, but the best that I can be for *myself.* I don't compare myself to others. My success is not in competition with anyone else's, and I am not keeping score between any teams but my own. If I can score a higher level each day and feel accomplished, based on my own score yesterday, then yes, that is a good indicator of growth. I do want to be the best, but for myself, my business, and my team. Not against anyone else.

Am I motivated by money? Yes, but not so I can buy myself tons of things that I will never take with me when I die. I really had to get my mind wrapped around the fact that money can be a good thing. The more money I have, the more I can give and the more I can do for others. So, I have prayed to my G.O.D. to thank Him for the success He has brought me because it is allowing me to serve others. Not only can I comfortably sleep at night and know that I am taking care of my home, my family, and our finances, I am able to give and help others through my experiences so they can achieve their own financial independence. So, there is no negative in that.

Do I really want the best and finest in everything? Yes, the best and finest in everything that I am willing to spend or in what I demand of myself and my team. "Do everything with a spirit of excellence unto Him" is another sentence I repeat to myself daily. Why would I not expect the best and finest of myself? Why does anyone deserve anything less than the finest and best I have to give?

So, do you see now how the way you look at things can completely transform your life? Yes, I am a powerful and successful woman, but one who has a huge heart and giving spirit and the best of intentions and has no desire to step on others to reach my level of desired success.

When you list the characteristics within yourself that maybe you are not most proud of, there is no shame to be had. You need to surface the characteristics that may have a negative vibe around them and simply change the way you think about them. Once you change the way you think about them, you will feel differently about them. When you feel differently, you will act differently and when you act differently, you will ultimately end up with different results.

As you begin your journey in business, it will serve you well to become your own best leader.

If you lead with a servant's heart, others will follow.

CHAPTER 11

Time to Get Moving

THE MARIPOSA EFFECT
A – Achieve Your Dream

This is the final step in the Mariposa Effect, and it's all about putting your ideas into action so you can get the results you're seeking.

I'm going to dive right into one of the most common programming phrases we are all familiar with because it's one you need to change your thought process on right away in order to achieve your dream.

I know you've heard the saying "knowledge is power," am I right? I think everyone has heard that at some point in their lives, probably multiple times.

I want to break this programming thought now. I hate to tell you, but knowledge is not power – only *applied* knowledge is power.

It does not matter how much you know, how smart you are, or how many skills and tools you have in your back pocket if you are not doing anything with them. If you are not applying every bit of knowledge, skill, smarts, and tools, they mean nothing. Ouch.

I'm sorry if that hurt, but, my friend, your dream is not a joke. Your potential is not a joke. Your future and how you want to spend your unique gift on earth is not a joke, so I'm okay with ouch moments.

We all know people who claim to be so smart and have an answer for everything yet are doing nothing.

Your broke Uncle Chuck will freely and openly give you advice on how to start your business and tell you that he read all about some of the best practices to implement right away in your business and what you should focus on first, etc. He'll tell you that you shouldn't do that, but it would be smart if you did this, but if he's your broke Uncle Chuck, he has probably not done anything with his knowledge. He hasn't applied all the great things he's read himself. There's no power in his knowledge, he hasn't applied it, and that's why he is broke and on the couch.

I don't care how smart you are. I don't care about how high your GPA is. I don't care how many degrees and certifications and pretty awards you have displaying your name. Yes, be proud of those things, but I am not impressed by them. They tell me nothing about the probability of success you'll have when it comes to starting your own business. If you continue to hide behind your fear and do not apply those wonderful accomplishments in your life, they mean nothing.

I may have just pissed you off, and I'm okay with that. That is just Mr. Ego peeking around the corner and he can leave any time. Here's the thing: you want me on your side because I know you can do it. I already believe in you.

You have what it takes but you must take what you have and do something with it.

Every accomplishment, skill, and experience you've gone through has taught you something, but what are you doing with it all? What you do is what makes the dream come true.

There are so many people out there who can roll out their list of degrees, but they are working hard for someone else. They are building someone else's dream. Yes, they collect a paycheck, but there is no freedom in building someone else's dream. You have your own unique dream to bring to life.

Don't get me wrong, if it is easier to simply go to work every day, do your job, and collect your paycheck, then do that. But I know you're here because you want different, and so I'm giving you things to think about and to get clear on so you can make the right choice for you and move forward with a clean "yes" or "no."

The next time you hear that phrase "knowledge is power," call it out. You now know better. Knowledge is not power. It doesn't matter what you know, it matters what you do with what you know. Apply the knowledge you have, and get to moving forward toward the life you desire.

Do this in the way that works for you. Do you know how to work with what is in harmony with you? I bet not because you probably can't even remember the last time you heard the word harmony!

I know, I feel you.

Here's the thing. Being in harmony with yourself is the surest way to take the knowledge you possess and apply it to gain amazing results.

Being in harmony with yourself is knowing how you think, behave, and create. These three elements, when brought together in harmony, will keep you feeling more like yourself than ever before while achieving more than you ever thought possible.

How you think is already different than when you first began reading this book. You know the power of your thoughts, and you know how to change your thinking in order to feel differently about something.

In order to begin working in harmony within yourself, pay attention to how you think, and be honest with yourself. If you find you are more of a negative thinking person, then priority number one is to begin changing that to positive thinking person. Make conscious effort each day to think in a positive manner on all things in your life.

Next, let's look at how you behave. If you were already a business owner, how would your behavior need to be improved upon? For example, are you going to continue to go out with your girlfriends on Friday night and post pictures of yourself with a drink in your hand, partying it up? Unless you're in the party and beverage business, probably not.

There are new things you will want to consider that you never did before. You want to project the image you want to be known for. You never know when an opportunity is going to present itself, so be ready.

I'll share one of my stories of "being ready."

I was in New York for a branding workshop. I had just got to my hotel and I was tired from traveling all day. My hair looked like a football helmet had exploded right on top of my head and I was beat. I wanted to get settled into my room, order room service, and relax before my intense training started the following day.

I called down to order room service and the gentleman on the telephone asked if he could call me back. Uhmmm, okay???

When my telephone rang, I answered, no one was there. A short while later, it rang again, and I answered. Again, no one was there. I was so confused.

By this time, almost an hour had passed, and I was starving. It wasn't late, I just didn't want to leave my room. I didn't want to make myself up and comb my hair, etc. but I kept hearing my G.O.D. tell me…go downstairs and eat.

So, like a little kid, dragging my feet and talking back to my inner voice, I said, "Fine, I'll just go down to eat really quick and come back up and relax." It was during the week, so it shouldn't be too busy down by the bar, I thought.

The bar was not busy. Nice, I could order my food, have a glass of wine, and disappear back to my room.

No kidding, in a matter of thirty minutes, the bar was full, there was an event being set up right next to where I was sitting, and a lady came and sat next to me. We started talking (she reminded me of one of my cousins). Anyway, we got to talking and she let me know that she was there to participate in a women's global networking event. What?

Next thing I know, I'm being introduced to a lady from Ireland, a lady from Texas, a lady from California. They were from all over and all I could think was, "I didn't put my lipstick on. Does my hair still look like an exploded football on my head? Why, God, why???"

But I held true to myself and talked about what I know best, business and leadership.

Fast forward to today. I am still friends with that group of women. I have since been a guest on one of the attendee's podcasts and invited as a guest speaker at an event, etc.

So, the opportunity served me well. I met very powerful and successful female entrepreneurs, gained some exposure and connections, and made new friends, all because God wouldn't let me order room service that night.

All the connections made that night over dinner were not even the reason I was in New York, so this is the reason why I say stay open to opportunities. They are around you all the time if you look for them.

I could have remained disappointed that I wanted to stay in my room and rest, but instead, I chose to be thankful that my room service didn't work out, and I gained some amazing relationships that night.

So, my friend, do yourself a favor and be ready for all the opportunities that are bound to come your way.

And the last component to being in harmony with yourself is to think about how you create.

This one can be a tricky one because some people don't even consider themselves creative. The truth is, everyone is creative. Creativity just looks different for different people.

Creativity, in this sense, means how and when do you come up with your best ideas? This goes back to when I asked earlier about getting your best work done, late at night or early in the morning. Some people need silence and others need background noise. Some prefer to use a planner in their phone, while others prefer a handwritten calendar to keep in their purse, etc.

Take some time to think about how and when you are most creative and do most of your work in that way. You'll get more done in shorter amount of time and have a sense of balance throughout your day.

In other words, once you determine how you think, behave, and create, you will be able to work in a way that is in harmony with you.

Don't get me wrong, problems will always come up. Sometimes these can be little and sometimes these can be big. But when you're working in harmony with yourself, you're better prepared to handle these situations. One thing to never lose sight of is that you can always change your plan, but do not change your dream.

You are growing every day. You are changing every day. So, basically, your plan will be outdated every day. You should be writing a new plan every day. That is why I don't want you looking too far ahead. You must have a vision, but you can only do one thing at a time. Do that one thing.

Again, change your plan, do not change your dream.

When my husband died of a heart attack at only forty-nine years old, I had a lot of people ask me, "Elena, what are you going to do now?" They knew I had left my corporate leadership position to focus on my business full-time, and so I understood why I was being asked that question.

Plus, I had two boys to take care of, a home, three dogs, and now all sorts of other stuff too, so I knew where that question was coming from.

I would answer, "What do you mean, what am I going to do now? I'm going to focus on my business full-time and continue on with my dream."

Just because life had come and hit me, and hit me hard, did not mean my dream should die. My dream was mine to have and it was my responsibility to breathe life into it. I was not going to give my dream the opportunity to come visit me at the end of my life and ask why I didn't pay attention to it.

I know exactly what I am to do and who I am to help, and so, when life kicked me in the booty for a moment, I changed my plan. I didn't work for a month, so I could sort through personal stuff, and then I got busy, in a new way.

I worked with intensity like never before. I had a new urgency behind helping my clients, because I had a whole new perspective on wasting time. I was more driven to help others live their dreams because I had experienced firsthand how quickly life can be gone.

So, my friend, I tell you, when things happen, change your plan, do not change your dream. I can't emphasize that enough!

Surround yourself with a power circle of people to help you though the challenges that will surface, especially in those times you are struggling the most.

I don't know how I would have gotten through my husband's death and continued serving others if I didn't have strong coaches in my life pushing me through my own pain. I had coaches, not family, helping me because they could be understanding of my rollercoaster of emotions without allowing me to hide behind excuses.

My husband may have died, but it did not mean that my dream had to die. I was still living. God had given me a gift. I still had to get up each day and function through the pain and do work. As a coach myself, I understand the power of having a strong coach in your life. I am so thankful for the coaches I have in my life because they kept me standing at a time when I thought my life was going to crumble to pieces.

These are the kind of people you want in your circle. The kind who will allow you to be broken, but will push you to become stronger.

Your power circle of people should ask how they can better support you and encourage you to stay the course when things get tough. Your power circle should not be your best friends, it should be leaders, coaches, mentors, or teachers who already have what you want. That have already traveled a journey of their own and have experience that will serve you well.

This journey of yours will be difficult, especially because there will be phases of growth where you will feel all alone.

This is going to sound nuts, but I want you to envision a bed of flowers starting to peek through the soil.

Beautiful colors are beginning to shine through, but only one flower is fed special food and receives special care. It grows rapidly. Next thing you know, the one single flower that receives special care and special food grows taller and stronger than all the other flowers around it.

This is going to happen to you. As you begin to grow and feed your mind and change your thinking and become focused, you are going to sprout up. If those around you don't choose to do the same thing themselves, they are not going to grow with you.

This is difficult, but keep on growing. Do your thing. You may find that some of your friendships will continue, and some will end. It is okay, this is part of the journey and part of your purpose. You cannot hold yourself back for fear of who might get left behind.

I remember at one time in my life, I had to remind myself that I couldn't feel bad for leaving behind those who I gave the opportunity to grow with me.

As you find others who are also working hard toward their dream, you'll establish new friendships, and those new friendships will bring with them new awareness. New awareness expands your potential.

What and who you know right now determines how far you can go. You can't go beyond where you are right now, unless you expand or grow your awareness.

Sort of like reading this book, you can take all these steps and lessons, but unless there is someone challenging your thinking from a different perspective, you will only see it and understand it from where you currently are.

Find those who can gently expand your awareness, because that is how your growth can happen at a rapid pace and get you to success that much sooner.

Are you ready to take your dream by the reins and pull it in? It's your responsibility to breathe life into it. Stop wasting precious time and get busy. You have what it takes.

CHAPTER 12

No Excuses Welcome Here

I f everyone believed they could start a business, they probably would. Who doesn't want time freedom, financial freedom, and to be their own boss? But not everyone believes they can.

Becoming aware of the success that resides within you is merely a simple act of inviting someone into your life who knows how to surface new awareness.

Think about it. You know what you know. You perceive things from your viewpoint. Unless you get someone else's viewpoint, you will never have a different perspective. You can only see what you see.

Think about a cloud floating softly in the sky. When you look at the cloud, at first glance all you see is a little white puff that looks like a cotton ball. But then, your best friend says, "That cloud looks like an elephant," you stare at it intently for a brief second, and suddenly, you're able to make out the shape and OMG, it does look like an elephant to you.

You can see it now. How did you not notice that before? How, just moments earlier, did you only see a little white puff that looked like a cotton ball?

Awareness, my friend. It's called awareness.

This is how awareness is expanded in your very own mind and how the answers already within you are brought to the surface. When someone else gives you a new way to look at things, you're able to see things differently.

It's not pushing their thoughts and beliefs on you, it's giving you another layer and another way to look at something.

So, I can confidently say that you have the answers within you, you just don't know them yet.

I also know there is one thing that will prevent you from taking any step forward or making any type of change. There is one thing you're guilty of, which is also the number one cause of failure, and it's not some radical belief or deep dark hidden secret, it's something so simple, you probably won't like the answer.

Here goes: if you don't make changes. If you don't take a chance on yourself. If you choose to remain stuck. If you fail, it is because of your own excuses! Ouch!

Excuses are the number one cause of failure, and I can't tell you how many dreams I have seen get thrown into the trash because of excuses.

Excuses are limitless and the more you attempt to remove them from your life, the more you will see that they are everywhere, and it will drive you frickin' nuts.

Right now, we could probably have a conversation, and I would be able to pull out several excuses of your own that you wouldn't consider to be excuses. This is because we are so saturated with listening to them and using them ourselves that we don't even detect them anymore. I find myself trying to pull excuses out of my back pocket when it's convenient, and I have to put myself in check real quick. Excuses will kill a dream, and quickly.

Excuses will prevent you from living with joy and passion. Excuses will prevent you from ever stepping out from behind that desk that is not your desk. Excuses will hold you down and prevent you from living your best life.

Excuses come in every shape and size. Here are the most common ones that I hear all the time. "I don't have money. I don't have time. My schedule doesn't allow it. My spouse isn't supporting me. I feel sick today. I don't know where to begin. If I get 'this' done first, then I will get to 'that.' What if I fail? What will people think?" OMG, this list goes on and on...

Think about some of the things popping up in your mind right now as to why you are not ready to move forward. I know there are several excuses in there.

Here's the thing though. To get what you want, you must make choices, not excuses.

Yes, maybe on the initial surface, you may think you don't have the money. How about we look at where all the money is being spent over a month's time? I can assure you, from past experiences, the money is there. You just choose to spend it on other things. Haircuts, hair color, manicures, pedicures, coffees, lunches, dinners, purses, cable TV, going out to the movies, taking the kids to dance, golf, vacations, etc.

The money is there, it's a choice if you choose to invest it on your growth or not. But don't lie to yourself and tell yourself you don't have it. That is an excuse.

I tried using the money excuse myself several times. The first time was in my direct sales marketing side job. I knew what it was going to cost up front and I really didn't have the money. I remember praying to my G.O.D. one night, shortly after my divorce, and being afraid because I didn't know where the money I needed was going to come from. I didn't want my boys to have to keep eating peanut butter and jelly sandwiches. Anyway, a friend of mine, who I hadn't seen or heard from in a while, texted me, right when I was asking my G.O.D. what I should do.

She texted me asking if I would come watch her put on a presentation at her new job. She was selling health supplements. I told her I would be there because I absolutely wanted to support her.

I went and I knew when the time came to sign people up, I was going to feel weird because I really didn't have the money to join or buy anything. But I knew in my heart that if I got in on this business of selling health supplements, I could make some additional cash. It was a good fit for me because I was a fitness trainer, and even though my business was good, it was never set up to support me through a divorce and immediately becoming a single mom.

When she asked me about joining her team or buying the program, I was honest with her and said I didn't have the money. Here's the thing…this might sound legit to you and not like an excuse, but let me show you how this was an excuse of mine and what happened next.

As I sat there for a moment, I remembered how her invitation via a text message came right at a time that I was praying and asking my G.O.D. to show me how I was going to get the money I needed. This was how I was going to get that money. He had placed in me in this position and I could recognize it and do something with it, or I could ignore it and go back to asking Him what to do.

I knew this was an opportunity and I should take it and figure out the rest later. So, I walked over to my friend and I told her. I was honest with her and I said, "I don't have the money to buy this today, but I want to do it because I know I have the potential to make a great deal of money. Can I borrow $96 from you right now, so that I can sign up and get started right away?"

Now, pride would have probably stopped a lot of people from doing what I did, and that's okay. But to me, it was fighting for my children and trusting in my G.O.D.

She said yes. I joined her team, with a small investment from her of $96. The next week, I hosted my first meeting to promote my health supplement product business and had her come and do the presentation because I was too new to know anything about the business, but made $2,400 in sales in one night. I paid her back her $96 that night, just a week from when I borrowed it.

If I had listened to my excuse of "I don't have the money" I wouldn't have generated an additional one to two thousand dollars biweekly for the next couple of years.

That's what excuses will do. They will tell you that you don't have it or that you can't do it, but that is not true. Sometimes you have to know that you can and do it; the details will come later.

The night I was praying, the night she texted me, changed my life and my G.O.D. answered my prayer, but I could have missed it with my own excuse.

The same goes with the excuse of time. You may tell yourself you don't have time, but you do if you choose to. Stop watching TV. Leave work on time. Let your family know that on Tuesday and Thursday, you're going to spend a couple hours investing in your learning and growth, so they know what to expect in advance. Tell your girlfriends you can't make it out for drinks after work. Let the kids know that, over the next few weeks, there will be no movie night or trips to the mall. Again, choices. Don't tell yourself you don't have time. If you don't want to invest the time, be honest with yourself. Don't fill your own head with your own excuses.

Yes, this may sound harsh, but it's the truth. I promised you that was all you'd get from me. It does nothing for me to lie to you. I want you to succeed. I want you living a life of freedom and on your terms. I'm doing it, so why not you?

You are your business' best asset. The business is not about the product or the service, it is about you and the connections you make with others.

There is nothing brand new out there, so for you to become successful, people will have to want to do business with you. Be the person you needed at one time in your life.

Trust your instincts. Listen to your inner voice. Believe that you are enough. The main reason most people don't break free and start a business of their own is they don't believe they can. If you won't bet on yourself, why should anyone else?

I remember one of the first things I had to overcome years ago was what people would think of me.

I supplemented my income with a few direct sales marketing side hustles…hey, everyone has a hustle at some point. I had the one I mentioned earlier, that was very successful for me. It was successful for me because I was all in. I used the products, I believed in them and I spoke from my heart when I talked about them. I was successful because I led the business with my heart…not the product.

I also had one that was not so successful, and it took me a while to figure out the reason why.

I believed in the products, but why wasn't anyone buying them from me? Because I didn't believe in myself this time around. I didn't go all in. I would tell myself, "If I can get so much in sales, then I will go all in."

It doesn't work that way. You must first go all in, and people will flock to you. You must believe in yourself enough to know that you are going to make it work, and it will.

I didn't know this years ago, and I really wish someone would have told me because I would have saved a lot of time and a lot of money. But sometimes the lessons you learn are an investment.

What I couldn't see is that my customers weren't just into the product, they were into supporting me and wanted to do business with me. I didn't see it and instead kept myself hidden behind the product, even though the product was available everywhere.

It took me a very long time to learn that people don't do business with you because of what you have to offer, they do business with you because of who you are.

So know yourself enough to know that you have what it takes, and invest in the things that will bring you to the highest level of yourself. That is what people want from you. That is what will make them want to support you and be your customer.

I know you're scared – that part is normal. You're looking change in the face and wondering if it's right for you. What if you go this way and it doesn't work? What if you go that way and you feel stuck every frickin' day of your life? You're at a crossroads now; there is no turning back. You're aware of new things and you can't hide from them. So, yes, it's scary.

I will tell you though, just decide. The moment you decide that, "Yes, I am going to turn right," or "Yes, I am going to turn left," you will be on a new path.

If your path is to embark on something brand new and learn more about what it takes to start a business, great, let's get started! And if your path is to tell yourself that right now is not the right time for you, own that decision and confidently walk into work on Monday and give it your all. At least you have given yourself fair opportunity to know the choice you are making for yourself is the right one for you.

No matter what it is that you do in life, do it with a spirit of excellence unto Him. You cannot go wrong in that case.

No matter where you are in your life, prosper where you are planted. Give it your all, right where you are.

What it all really comes down to is "be happy." Life is short, live it. You are not promised tomorrow, do your best today. Nothing is easy, so pick what is worth fighting for, and give this world the best version of you.

Bet on yourself and allow yourself a few short weeks to discover what it is you truly want.

Make an educated decision, don't just guess on what is best for your future.

Do the work, quit with the excuses, and feel confident in your next move.

CHAPTER 13

Broken Stronger Boss in the Making

As you ponder on the decision of whether you are ready to become your own boss, I want to encourage you to walk in faith.

You already know what it is that you want to do. No one can tell you what is right or wrong; only you know what is best for you and what your inner voice is telling you. Trust it. It knows you best.

The main thing to keep in mind is that this decision is yours to make. You are unique. You are one of a kind. You have a distinct purpose that no one knows besides you and your G.O.D.

Do what you know is the right thing for you, and all the other pieces will come together.

Begin by placing the intentional focus on your desire. You now know this is entirely different than wishing for something.

Listen to your inner voice. This is where your truth lies. Don't hide from it, and don't try to negotiate with it. It is pure, and it's coming from your highest source. Trust it.

Stop hiding behind false layers of perfection. No one is perfect, and we all deserve to see your greatness. Allow yourself to flex your muscles and share your strength.

Face the obstacles that are blocking you from reaching your highest potential. Fear has no place when it comes to moving forward and living your dream.

Take power over the design of your future, and think differently in all things. You know the power that your thinking has over your life. Begin to make the changes you seek.

Learn the value of understanding others, and make the connections that will last a lifetime. Success depends on people, and you have what it takes to make the ultimate connections.

Lead others with confidence and ease. You know that leadership is not about being a bossy boss. Take pride in your ability to lift others up as you rise to your own higher level of success.

You're ready. Put your ideas into action and get the results you desire. You have all that is required to succeed at whatever it is you put your mind to.

I know after going through my eight non-negotiable steps in the Mariposa Effect, you are already a changed person. Take some time to get to know this new version of her and allow her to grow.

There is no time for others to keep pushing down your potential or shutting off your greatness. None. Begin today to let your brilliance shine because the world needs to see more of her.

You know you are capable, and you know you are worthy; it's time to let God's love flow through you so you can share that same love with others. You are not meant to sit behind a desk that is not meant for you.

Do not be afraid to take inventory of all the crap you have been through in life; let it serve you well in this very moment. You have the strength to move forward. You have the strength to create change and design the life you want to live for you and your family and to change your legacy.

One of the things I learned early on is that when a passion is within you, there is no shutting it down. You may tuck it behind problems, you may tuck it behind excuses, but it will surface and will show up in all sorts of ways in your life.

It will come out as anger, as frustration, as depression, as silence, as gossip, all sorts of things that don't put a smile on your face. The world needs your smile.

Whether now is the time for you or not, know that there will come a time and it will be perfect for you. I hope you are ready to make your decision because life is short.

Have a dream? Live it.

Love someone? Tell them.

Not happy? Change something.

Whatever it is in your life that you feel is holding you back, remove it now because you are meant to be shared.

We all want to be wanted. We all want to know that what we are doing is making a difference. We are not here to take up space and take up air and not contribute anything back.

The ideas you have floating around in your head are meant to be shared, and your dream is meant to be lived

Live it.

If you have failed in the past, good for you. Learn from it, use it, and go again.

You have read this book, you have gone through the Mariposa Effect, and you have learned eight non-negotiable steps to improve yourself all around and help you determine if starting a business is the right decision for you.

Know that you have everything you need to walk in faith toward your freedom and excellence, but only you can take the next step.

You're ready, so go get it.

Acknowledgments

First, I want to thank my gorgeous angel for loving me and supporting me from heaven. His lessons in life have taught me that there is no better time to do anything than now. I miss you, sweetheart. I will always love you. May God continue to work on us, through us, and for us. I'm proud of you.

To my boys, my loves, my world, my joy, and my hope. You both have been my strength and provided a solid foundation for me to continue fighting for my dream. You have been my greatest cheerleaders and have given me the determination to never give up. You provide a safe place for me to shed my tears and aren't embarrassed to give your mama hugs when she needs them (you don't even know how special that makes me feel). I can't express enough how proud of the both of you I am, and how honored I am that God chose me to be your mother. I love you both with every ounce of my being.

Josiah, you have an incredible future ahead of you and a talent that is God-given. Never stop reaching for your dreams and do not ever let anyone make you think you can't. You can and you will. I look forward to being your first date at the Grammys, my son.

Manny, you are a beautiful spirit and so frickin' intelligent it scares me at times. I can't wait to see where life takes you. You will succeed at anything you set out to do because you already do everything with a spirit of excellence. Do not ever change. Stay true to who you are because you are pretty amazing, my son!

My beautiful mother, my forever date and real-life hero. Thank you for listening to me and reminding me of my strength even when I feel I have misplaced it. You are the best example of what never giving up looks like. I am thankful for you every day and appreciate you in all things…and, you just happen to be the best grandma ever! I love you, Mama.

My beautiful sister, I love you too much! You are strength, sacrifice, faith, and love all wrapped up into one beautiful spirit. You are the most selfless person I know, and I thank you for always listening and laughing with me! I love you, Sissy.

My beautiful mother-in-law, Carole, I love you. Thank you for always supporting me and receiving me into your life as your daughter from day one. It has been a true joy of mine to see you shine. Your faith is contagious, and the love you have for others is a blessing.

To my fellow Broken Stronger Boss Ladies, the QI team – you rock! Thank you for making a difference in my life and allowing me to make a difference in yours.

Thank you to Angela Lauria and The Author Incubator's team, as well as to David Hancock and the Morgan James Publishing team for helping me bring this book to print.

Thanks for Reading

When I talk to women, one of the most common issues they report is that they don't even remember what a dream is. They don't know how to put into words what they truly desire out of life. They have forgotten what they are good at, what brings them joy, and what sparks their energy.

Forget about being at a point of starting a business, they don't really have anything they are passionate about anymore, and they certainly aren't clear on their purpose.

This happens when years are spent caring for everyone else, and there's nothing left for yourself. It's not a reflection of anyone's strength, it's merely a wake-up call that it is time to put intentional focus on self-care and rediscovery.

Because of the astonishing high rate of "lost women," I have put together a special training class to help "Reveal Your Purpose." Find it here: https://www.brokenstronger. life/reveal-your-purpose.

Check it out and let me know what you think on your favorite social media site.

About the Author

Elena Zehr is a successful certified life coach, transformational development trainer, and motivational speaker who helps women break free from self-limiting beliefs and become CEOs over their lives by equipping them with tools to design the future they've always imagined.

She empowers women to regain confidence and trust in themselves and become witness to their own strength as they watch their lives transform before their very eyes.

Elena became certified in coaching, speaking, and training through the John Maxwell Team and revolutionized her training. Now, Elena combines years of entrepreneurial expertise alongside key corporate leadership skills with an inclusion of spiritual strengthening, which allows for complete life transformation. Her signature quote is, "Healing is the foundation dreams are built upon."

As a recipient of the Women's Entrepreneurial Leadership Recognition Award presented by the Northeast Indiana Innovation Center, Elena has devoted the past seventeen years of her life to lifting others to excellence and leadership.

She develops individualized plans for her clients to release and overcome the limiting beliefs preventing them from living their true purposes in life. She also develops exclusive curricula for her clients who prefer to work in small group settings to provide opportunity for maximum growth and create quality connections.

Elena loves taking care of her two teenage sons and three dogs. Her favorite things are angels, collecting crosses from every city she visits to display on a cross wall in her home, and lipstick. She feels every girl needs that one perfect shade of red.

Website: https://www.brokenstronger.life

Email: Elena@brokenstronger.life

Facebook: https://www.facebook.com/brokenstronger

CPSIA information can be obtained
at www.ICGtesting.com
Printed in the USA
JSHW021641300620
6407JS00003B/90